CAUGHT IN THE CROSSFIRE

Encountering God
on the Battlefield of the Heart

Joyce Strong

HORIZON BOOKS

A DIVISION OF CHRISTIAN PUBLICATIONS, INC.
CAMP HILL, PENNSYLVANIA

HORIZON BOOKS

A Division of Christian Publications, Inc.
3825 Hartzdale Drive, Camp Hill, PA 17011
www.cpi-horizon.com

ISBN: 0-88965-160-4
© 1999 by Horizon Books
All rights reserved
Printed in the United States of America

99 00 01 02 03   5 4 3 2 1

THANKS

To my husband Jim, my champion and best
earthly friend through the perils of this life.

Contents

Part 1: Pierced by Conviction

Part 2: Shadows of Resistance

PART 3: FINAL VICTORY

FOREWORD

*C*aught in the Crossfire is a book about the heart. Joyce Strong understands the human heart with its self-centered focus, hidden shame, shattered dreams—and yet, its deep yearning and incredible hunger for more of the presence of God.

Caught in the Crossfire brings alive the men and women of Scripture in their humanity and their redemption, and portrays their same struggles in the portraits of contemporary lives.

But most importantly, Joyce Strong understands the heart of God—always reaching toward us, always loving, always forgiving, always offering a second chance. Our problem is not really temptation or a specific sin—it is surrender! When we finally come to the end of ourselves and raise our battle-wearied arms and scarred hearts to Him, the divine exchange takes place. My unrighteousness for His righteousness!

This book came to me as my own heart was crying out for a deeper walk with God. As I read it, I found myself once again awed by the amazing grace and purpose of God, and audibly assenting, "Yes! Yes!"

Caught in the Crossfire reminds us that "whosoever will may come" and then invites us into the presence of the King. I highly recommend it!

Terry Meeuwsen
Co-host, *The 700 Club*

PREFACE

There is a deep hunger within the body of Christ for the presence of God. While many of us have been carefully keeping up appearances, our hearts now recognize that things are not as they should be between us and Him. We can't hear His voice as clearly as we could in the beginning. We are frustrated . . . and frightened.

In the midst of our struggle, the crimson silhouette of the cross seems etched into every sunset. It reminds us of a day when we loved only the Lord, when whatever He said we would do. We remember how clean we felt, how close to heaven, how totally accepted and affirmed by God. But we have, perhaps, let so many things, so many loves draw us away from our devotion to Him.

And God's answer to our cry is to set us precisely within the crossfire of the Holy Spirit's conviction. We begin to see beyond our circumstances into the dark areas of resistance that have become entrenched in our lives. It is into those shadows that the Holy Spirit is aiming His fire. He knows that without complete surrender, we can never be intimate with God. Intimacy is that for which we were created, and without which we will be miserable.

He hears our cry and sees our hunger, and He loves us. As we find ourselves caught in the crossfire, may we yield control to Him at last. Then, how clearly will we hear His voice again, how sweet will be His presence!

INTRODUCTION

On the following pages you will meet men and women throughout time who were caught in the crossfire, who were challenged by the Lord to obey and trust Him alone. The reward of His presence was always worth the pain to their flesh—when they chose to surrender. The losses when they did not obey were truly tragic.

I pray that you and I, when in the same situations, will turn to Him in obedience. I pray that we will repent instantly and forgive quickly when faced with our own sins and others' offenses. I pray that we will absorb the Holy Spirit's healing when we let Him probe the depths of our lives and expose the ways in which we have left the Father's presence in our attempt to heal ourselves.

Most of all I pray that we will learn to *live* in His presence daily, being obedient because we love Him so, not needing the fire of conviction hot upon us so very often to keep us close to Him.

Elijah's ancient question pierces us today: "How long will you waver between two opinions?" (1 Kings 18:21).

And with Joshua may we reply, "As for me and my household, we will serve the LORD" (Joshua 24:15).

The stories in this book are taken from real-life composites of many who, like me, have been or are now caught in the crossfire.

PART 1:

PIERCED BY
CONVICTION

CHAPTER ONE

SURRENDER OF EXPECTATIONS

Although the Lord gives you the bread of adversity and the water of affliction, your teachers will be hidden no more; with your own eyes you will see them. Whether you turn to the right or to the left, your ears will hear a voice behind you, saying, "This is the way; walk in it."
(Isaiah 30:20-21)

The damp walls closed in on the lone prisoner, the icy stone floor sending bone-chilling shards of pain through his feet, ankles and up along his spine. An involuntary shudder ran through his body as he shifted from one numb foot to the other; the simple skin tunic he wore offered no consolation from the cold.

The numbness of his body spread to his will, while his mind rambled over the rocky terrain of his unusual life.

"I had not expected this!" John the Baptist whispered as he rubbed his eyes with fingers stiff from the cold. Leaning heavily against the rough wooden door of his cell, he began questioning the shadows that played about the corners of the dim underground cubicle. "Why am I still locked up?" he asked. "If He is the Messiah, why hasn't He come for me?"

Despair crept into his voice. "Why does He permit the wicked to live on and rule? What manner of Savior is this?"

No Ordinary Fellow

In this singular moment, John may seem quite insignificant. But this prisoner is no ordinary fellow. Born by divine decree to Elizabeth, who had been barren, and Zechariah, a priest before the Lord, John had a unique purpose. He was chosen to be the prophet and forerunner of the Messiah, the one to announce Christ's coming and instruct the people on sin and repentance.

This he had done when people sought him in the wilderness. He continued to do it before the wicked Herod, who had not appreciated his message. And so, John landed in prison.

He remembered his speeches to the religious leaders—back when he was charging about the countryside preaching and baptizing all who would believe in Jesus as the Messiah. "The ax is already at the root of the trees, and every tree that does not produce good fruit will be cut down and thrown into the fire!" He had been so confident about justice coming in his time. But now he was not so sure.

Slowly shaking his head, he wondered, *When will Jesus destroy such vermin as Herod, whose own sin has demanded my imprisonment?* He sank to the foul-smelling floor, disregarding the greater pain its cold would bring to his joints. He wondered aloud, "Is He, after all, the Christ? Or will there be another who will bring evil to its knees?" *(Taken from Matthew 3:1-12; 11:1-6; 14:1-12.)*

Yielded to God's Plan

Before ever seeing the cross, John was beheaded. He died with only the consolation of a simple message from Jesus:

"The blind receive sight, the lame walk, those who have leprosy are cured, the deaf hear, the dead are raised, and the good news is preached to the poor. Blessed is the man who does not fall away on account of me" (Matthew 11:5-6).

The first part came from Isaiah's well-known prophetic description of the Messiah. By sending John this passage, Jesus knew John would regain his perspective. He would see clearly once again that Jesus truly was the Messiah and that all was not lost. But it was the last statement that spoke most to John. This gentle plea from his beloved Jesus—to allow God to act as He will—kept him stalwart even under the blade of Herod's executioner. For a moment John's comprehension of fairness had been challenged by the pain of following Jesus. And so is ours today. How will we respond?

SUDDEN REVERSALS

Mark and Marie Thomas had worked hard to build a television ministry that would bring respect and glory to God. While great energy and prayer daily went into giving their viewers quality programming, at the same time they were careful not to neglect their children. Jody and Melissa, their twelve- and nine-year-olds, were doing well in school as a result and neither showed the slightest hint of the rebellion that all parents fear as their kids near their teen years. Life wasn't always easy, but it was sweet for Mark and Marie, and they didn't want anything to change.

Then Marie began having mysterious headaches. After three weeks of bouts with the pain, Mark took her to see Doc Johnson, their family physician. After running several routine tests and trying different headache medicines—all to no avail—he ordered an MRI.

"Mark, I'm scared," Marie cried into his shoulder as they sat close together in the hospital waiting room before the scheduled MRI.

"Honey, don't worry! There are folks all over the country praying for you. Nothing's going to go wrong. You'll see!" He wrapped his strong arms around her and held her to him.

Tilting her face up to his, she kissed him gratefully. He was always so confident. She needed his reassurance now more than ever.

After Marie went in for the MRI, Mark numbly watched the minutes tick away on the clock mounted over the receptionist's window. The nightmare would soon be over, he was sure.

But it had only begun. A malignant tumor had been growing for some time behind Marie's right eye, and operating would be risky. But, in the natural, it was their only choice. The prayers continued to rise from thousands of homes across the country—and from Mark's heart. He felt that his life would be over if Marie didn't make it, as surely as if the tumor were in his own body.

LITTLE HOPE

She survived the operation, but doctors were not able to remove all the malignancy. They held out little hope that Marie would recover. Radiation and chemotherapy only made her drift farther from life day by day. Meanwhile Mark was losing his grip. All the confident claims that he had made on television now echoed hollowly in his mind. Even though the show had to go on, he dreaded it more each day.

DOUBTS

"Whatever made me think I could preach, Dad?" he asked his father one night as they sat together over coffee. "The viability of everything I've ever claimed about God's power and goodness seems trashed by Marie's suffering." Then in a tone tinged with anger and bewilderment he questioned his father again. "Where is God when I need Him?"

He held his head in his hands, his fingers rubbing his temples in their attempt to drive away the distress and fear that consumed him. "It just isn't fair!" he finally blurted out.

His dad didn't know how to answer. Their eyes met, tears running down their faces.

"I've never experienced suffering like this!" Mark whispered. "I don't know if I can go on! I used to have all the answers, but now I have none. Where's my faith now? Where is my strength? After all we have done for Him, why won't He rescue us now?"

NOT A GAME

Life *is* often hard, but since we have given our lives to make Him known, shouldn't we be treated more fairly?

While we begin our Christian life gallantly, our vision tends to grow narrow on the journey. We start on our knees at the cross in surrender, then too easily rise to make the most of it. Our spiritual service, begun purely, often becomes our identity—for which we believe we deserve praise and deliverance from trouble.

We cry for fairness but it is nowhere to be seen. We are tempted to ask, "Is this some kind of game that God is playing?"

"Never!" comes the answer from the heavens. "Though you are often caught playing games with *Me*!" the thunder rolls. "You *do* to *get* all too often and then call 'foul!' when things don't go your way. Do you want reward on this earth only?" He seems to ask through the storm.

JUSTICE VS. FAIRNESS

God *isn't* fair, and He offers no apology.

But He is *just*. He is, in fact, the divine Justifier. He allows into our lives exactly what we need to bring us back to the cross and to deepen our intimacy with Him.

He knows that no amount of fairness will bring conviction of sin or change selfish hearts. All the fairness on this earth cannot prevent one person from becoming independent and drifting away from His precious presence.

He faced the blackness of death Himself so that we might live by His life. The great expense of that gift challenges us to go below the surface of things and yield to the deeper purposes of our lives . . . but not to cling too tightly to those lives, for they belong to Him. Until we learn this, we think Satan has won when the dungeon comes. We cry out, "Is Jesus truly the Christ, or should we look for another?" The truth is that Satan is merely at his wit's end. All the while, God is using even Satan's assault to do us good—if again we look for His resurrection power in the midst of our suffering.

The crisis for us is not the dungeon—and it wasn't for John. The crisis is in how we *respond* to the dungeon. If we judge God and allow bitterness to take root, we will truly be imprisoned. We will lose our freedom and the ability to see the light of day because our gaze has shifted from His face to what we expect of Him. Slowly our memory of His love will grow dim, and His lordship will be nearly lost.

"Blessed is the man who does not fall away on account of me" (Matthew 11:6).

LOSING TO WIN

Marie died gracefully but in terrible pain. It seemed a great relief to her when the end came. But before it did, she gently begged Mark to hold fast to his faith in God. To please her, he promised he would. But he had not the slightest idea how to keep that promise. After her death, his staff ordered him to take a three-month leave of absence from the ministry; they would not accept his resignation.

THE STRUGGLE

Daily Mark wrestled with God. He wanted to know why Marie had not been healed, but God offered no explanation. Instead, the Holy Spirit began piercing Mark's heart every time he was alone.

"Was Marie the reason you trusted Me when you gave your life to Me years ago? Were the blessings on your ministry the source of your strength as you began serving Me?" the Voice gently probed night after night.

Finally, Mark understood. In a solemn act, he knelt by the desk in his study late one evening after the kids were in bed. There he began his most honest prayer in a long, long time.

"Lord, I have loved my life and the blessings of family and ministry more than I have loved You. I come to You as I did in the beginning, with empty hands and no demands. I just want Your presence to be with me again as it was when I met You and first felt Your love."

Tears welled up in Mark's eyes. "Just let me see life with Your eyes and feel those around me with Your heart, please. I can't do this alone! Take my life and fill me with Your Spirit, then do with it as You will. *You* are my reason for living! *Your* presence only must again be my strength."

He slowly rose from his knees and went to bed. For the first time since Marie's death, he slept soundly.

In His Presence Again

A subtle change began to appear in Mark's behavior. He was quieter, more contemplative, more sensitive to the suffering of others. Privately he began praying again for others—often with unusual results.

He also wondered a great deal. He wondered at the peace stealing into his spirit even while his mind continued to ask questions of God. He spent more time with Jody and Melissa—listening attentively, seeing with tender eyes into the depths of their hearts. He wept with them and together they began to heal. They replayed the sweet times, more and more often imagining what Mommy might be doing now in heaven. She seemed to belong there, and life slowly slid back into focus for Mark and the children.

Mark had not realized how far from God he had drifted, even in the midst of ministry. He hadn't heard God's voice since early in his Christian experience, and in all the excitement of success, he hadn't missed it until Marie's death. But now he made daily trips to the foot of the cross to receive grace; there he poured out his faith, frustrations and doubts and he began to hear God's voice again.

RESTORED DEVOTION

Never had the Spirit of God spoken to him so gently as during those dark days after Marie's death. How could he have managed before without it? How wise of Marie to make him promise to hold fast to his faith in God! There wasn't much left at the time, but it had been enough to keep bitterness at bay so that he could hear the Holy Spirit's voice.

DEEPER PURPOSE

Our lives on this earth are precious, yet they are expendable—but only because they are wonderfully eternal! In the scheme of eternity, time does strange things: A thousand days may be as a breath, while a moment may last forever. God, and our spirits as well, are not locked into time and space, and He calls us to understand that. His commitment to us is eternal, and so must ours be to Him.

And our loving Father knows that if we gained the whole world but lost our first love for Him, we'd be desperately miserable in the end! So He draws us back. How faithful He is!

Our journey here is for one purpose—to learn to live by *His* life, not our own, and to experience the kind of intimacy with Him that will fill eternity. We will then be able to make Him known to others who have lost their way in the struggle of life. We begin to realize that we are not of this world and our faces turn toward heaven. Earth is but the battleground.

Rejection, reversals, disasters—especially when we are innocent—bond us to the suffering Savior. The cross embraced gives us a new heart—His heart! Therein is great compassion born. His voice teaches us not how to control our circumstances, but the mercy and favor of His presence. He is preparing us for service of a deeper nature than we ever knew when things were going "well."

11

COMPLETE SURRENDER

We knew before that following Him would cost us. But we thought that the sacrifice would be this world's glamour and riches, not our very lives! We learn, however, that circumcision of the heart is much more profound than of the flesh. It removes every remnant of control and earthly expectations, leaving us seemingly lifeless at His feet. Then His mercy takes over, quietly restoring us to Him once again. When earth is released, heaven is found.

Amazingly, when others encounter our surrendered lives, they begin to long for His presence too! We then have the priceless privilege of taking them home to the God who loves them as well.

CHAPTER TWO

ABSOLUTE TRUST

"For I know the plans I have for you," declares the LORD, "plans to prosper you and not to harm you, plans to give you hope and a future." (Jeremiah 29:11)

As the sun rose in the east, elusive early morning shadows played about the rugged crown of Mt. Moriah. It was now just a day's journey away. Abraham searched its dim outline for understanding as sand shifted beneath his sandaled feet.

The words of Jehovah, spoken clearly to him two days earlier, echoed again and again through his mind. They caused the old man's heart to pound.

THE CHALLENGE

"Abraham!" God called.

"Here I am," he replied, his heart rising with anticipation at the sound of the Lord's voice.

"Take your son, your only son, Isaac, whom you love, and go to the region of Moriah," God began.

Ah, what mighty revelation will there be this time? Abraham thought excitedly.

God continued. "Sacrifice him there as a burnt offering on one of the mountains I will tell you about."

Abraham gasped for air, barely able to breathe. He spent the night on his face before God.

PREPARATION FOR SACRIFICE

The next morning he cut wood for the fire and strapped it to the back of his best donkey. Provisions for the trip bulged from the pouches hanging down on the beast of burden. By the time the sun rose above the horizon, he, Isaac and two servants were on their way. By nightfall they would reach the mountain.

Abraham spoke in low tones to his servants. "Stay here with the donkey while I and the boy go over there," he said simply, motioning toward the mount in the distance. "We will worship and then we will come back to you."

The men obligingly prepared to remain at the campsite after strapping the wood for the sacrifice onto Isaac's back.

With provisions and a jug of water tied to the leather belt around his waist, Isaac was ready. He looked to his father for further directions. Taking the fire that they had brought with them, the old man nodded to Isaac to continue on with him.

Beginning to ascend the foothills, Abraham's thoughts went back in time. As his heart raced at the memories, he stumbled over a jagged stone in the path. Isaac grabbed Abraham's arm and steadied the ancient patriarch, while kicking the offending stone out of the way.

"Father, be careful, or you won't make it to the place of sacrifice." Isaac said to him gently.

Regaining his footing, Abraham clasped Isaac's hand, seemingly needing his son's steadying influence to keep him on course over the rugged terrain. Isaac smiled. There was a bond between this father and son that surpassed words and even actions, so sure was their love for one another.

THEIR SPIRITUAL HISTORY

While Abraham had taught Isaac animal husbandry and the management of vast material resources, he had doubly taught his son to listen for the voice of God and to obey Him utterly. Long ago he had told the boy of his own encounters with God and of God's promises concerning the great nation that would come through Isaac.

Isaac had believed every word. There wasn't the slightest doubt in the young man's heart that the Sovereign God was good and that He would fulfill His promises. Besides, he had the visible presence of his father to reflect God's goodness, and he trusted him completely.

Rarely had Abraham forced obedience from Isaac. This son had a profound sense of the future, a sense that all would be well if he stayed in Jehovah's hands and in obedience to his beloved father. He had come to understand that even the most unpleasant or difficult tasks had a purpose.

Abraham's history of trust had not been so illustrious. He had been a fearful man who, when in danger, took the path of least resistance. But now, if the future of the world were really to rest upon his shoulders, issues of self-preservation and control must be settled.

"Father?" Isaac broke through Abraham's reverie.

"Yes, my son?" Abraham replied.

"The fire and wood are here," Isaac said, "but where is the lamb for the burnt offering?"

Pain shot through Abraham's soul as he looked into the searching eyes of his beloved son.

"God will provide, Isaac. God will provide." *(Taken from Genesis 22:1-19.)*

ABRAHAM COMES OF AGE

How do we come to the place where our trust is so complete that we find no contradiction in a God Who tells us He loves us, and then instructs us to give up all that we hold most dear? How could Abraham have bound his precious son of promise—the very one through whom God had said He planned to bless the world—to the altar stones? How could a gentle, loving, faithful father have raised the blade above his head, prepared to plunge it into the heart of his dear son?

What changed Abraham from a coward—a man who had always questioned God's provisions—to a giant of the faith? What transpired in Abraham's heart that caused him to trust God beyond reason?

Perhaps like Isaiah (who would come generations later), Abraham really saw *himself* on the way to Moriah that day. Maybe he stumbled, not over God's command, but because of the revelation of his own sin in doubting God so often in the past. Perhaps, as he trudged along that rocky path, he was overcome by a deep conviction that God's plan was greater and farther-reaching than his mind could ever measure.

Did Abraham have an inkling of Mt. Moriah's role in the years to come? Could he have known that David would dream of a place of surrender there—the temple that his son Solomon would build? Did God whisper to him that someday His own Son would be on trial on this mountain for saying that He was the Son of Promise as well? Had Abraham felt the heavenly Father's pain over His own Son's impending death, and subsequently found the grace to be obedient?

Abraham came of age spiritually that day on Mt. Moriah. He left the wilderness and crossed over Jordan in his own life. He left behind all that had been a comfort to him and willingly surrendered the identity that could have been established through his son. He refused to yield even to his own heart.

He trusted God. In the moment he raised the knife and looked to heaven, he must have died a thousand deaths—not just his own, but for all of Isaac's descendants. He died to earthly logic, to human demands, to all that others would ever think of him. He went to the cross before it was ever invented, and he died. His selfishness was at last crucified. He became nothing; God was all that mattered. The cost of obedience was accepted—and paid. We know Abraham today as a great man of faith.

God counted it as righteousness and provided a substitute—a ram caught in the thicket near the altar.

THE PAIN OF SURRENDER

God omnisciently knew that Abraham would be obedient, willing even to kill his beloved son. He knew that the ram would be provided at the last moment and that Isaac would not die.

But neither father nor son knew for sure. They had no immediate indication that they would be spared the prescribed agony. True, they had options. Isaac could have overpowered his aged father and run. Abraham could have refused to even begin the journey to Mt. Moriah. But they didn't. They had no outward sign that God would change His mind. The death to all *had* to occur, paid in spiritual blood. The walk to the cross—and its acceptance—had to be made. The fact that, as Abraham reasoned, God could raise the dead (see Hebrews 11:19) made it no less a death.

The resulting pain was real for this father and son. I can't help but imagine the cries of grief and fear from both of them as Abraham felt the coldness of the blade, and Isaac saw it poised above his own body.

For us, too, the pain of total surrender is real. Death to life as we want to fashion it must occur.

Independence and self-sufficiency, controlling tactics, clinging to outcomes must die. Whether in relationships, ministry dreams, personal identity, expectations for family members, physical strength or money—all the good and bad of each—we must experience death to find freedom and intimacy with God.

And how do we give up dreams that roar in our bones, especially those that will obviously minister to others? How do we live with the prospect of dreams and gifts being abandoned forever? Who are we without them?

AMY'S DREAM

Music has been Amy's life. From the time she was big enough to climb up onto the piano bench and reach the keyboard, her fingers have sought to connect new melodies awaiting in the ivory keys with lyrics from her heart.

As a teenager in the sixties, she and two friends formed a trio, traveling in their own bus and cutting gospel records. Ministering the gospel in song was her greatest joy. With her parents cheering her on, she anticipated a career in music.

Then came marriage and three children. The tours stopped and the group split up. The church piano became her ministry platform. While her days and nights were spent in loving and nurturing her family, the dream of performing publicly again remained bound in the back of her life.

The songs still came, the words consigned to a notebook and the melodies stowed away in her memory. They were good songs that encouraged others to more fully know the love of God. A wrestling match ensued.

As she folded laundry and cleaned the house, she badgered God for an answer.

"When will the world hear these songs—when I'm old and gray and barely able to carry a tune?" Amy muttered to Him over and over as the years wore on. "I want to sing these songs for Your glory! They stand for who You and I are together. Do You want them to rot away in oblivion?" she said with disgust and frustration. Only silence greeted her grumbling . . . until one day He answered.

"Amy, do you love Me?" the Lord asked her gently. In shock she stopped stirring the stew and laid down the ladle.

"Yes, Lord. Just listen to my songs. They say so. They're my offering to You," came Amy's answer straight from her heart.

He pressed on. "Which do you love more, child, Me . . . or the music?"

Before she could answer, He asked another question. "Amy, do you think that You and I would be any closer if you could perform your music for others? Does our relationship *need* the songs in your notebook?"

"But my music is *me*, Lord. How can I come to You without it?" she asked, bewildered.

"No, your music is a gift—a gift from Me to you, not from you to Me," He answered her. "First there was you. And it is you I have always loved and you for whom I died. It is *you* I long to be with and bless. The songs are not so important, are they?"

Amy had no answer. Tears filled her eyes. In that moment of revelation she saw what she hadn't seen for forty-six years. She *did* perhaps love her music more than God. The gift had obscured the Giver.

Test of Love

Perhaps she was afraid to be alone with Him without the music. Had she feared that He wouldn't love her without it?

He spoke to her spirit again. "What will you do if I never make a way for you to record your songs? What if you die with them still tucked away in your memory and little notebook? Will you have loved Me any less, or I, you?"

"But Lord," Amy insisted through her tears, "I'm nothing without these songs. I'm just Amy—a nobody. My music is all I have to leave behind."

"When your children think lovingly of you, is it because of some song you wrote? And your husband—does he ask for your music or your heart when you're alone in the candlelight?

"Let the dreams go, Amy, let them go. Give them to Me. If I never grace your heart with another song, My passion for you will not lessen."

Amy wept as she listened.

"Don't you know that if your voice were silenced and no pianos remained on earth for you to play, I'd still sing love songs to you?" He continued to speak gently into her spirit. "You have thought that the music is born out of your love for Me. On the contrary, Amy, the music has been born out of My love for you!

"Will you accept My love songs and simply let them be between you and Me?"

Amy fell to her knees in her kitchen. The cross pierced her heart, letting all the insecurities and striving flow out and onto her Lord. Sweet silence enveloped her as she emptied herself at His feet. There on the floor she died to forty-some years of hopes and dreams. Then the sweetest melody she had ever heard poured into her soul! But she didn't run to write it down. There on her knees, she simply loved the Giver of the song.

OUR MT. MORIAH

As we seek the heart of God, each of us must travel to our own Mt. Moriah. We will love Him more dearly at the journey's end—whether there is a ram caught in the thicket or not.

CHAPTER THREE

AN UNDIVIDED HEART

Teach me your way, O LORD,
  and I will walk in your truth;
give me an undivided heart,
  that I may fear your name.
I will praise you, O Lord my God,
  with all my heart;
I will glorify your name forever.
For great is your love toward me;
  you have delivered me from the
    depths of the grave.
                    (Psalm 86:11-13)

The fire, hot upon his hands and face, fought against the cold that pressed upon his back. Out of the corners of his eyes, first to the left and then to the right, Peter sized up the servants and leaders who flanked him at the fire in the high priest's courtyard. For a brief moment he felt like one of them—unmarked and unhunted.

Inside, the high priest Caiaphas was questioning Jesus. The days of miracles and "hosannas" seemed far away—as if they were from someone else's past. Reality was the religious world in which Caiaphas and his men enforced the traditions that had governed Peter's people for centuries. Peter's heart pounded when he thought of Caiaphas turning on him personally. "I'm just a fisherman," he said to himself, wishing he were casting nets at this moment into the Sea of Galilee. In this courtyard his fear of what these men could do to him seemed to pale his love for Jesus.

What's taking Jesus so long? he wondered nervously. *It's nearly dawn!* Peter involuntarily put his hand over his heart. He feared that its pounding would soon give him away.

One man around the fire, a relative of the man whose ear Peter had cut off back in the Garden of Gethsemane, studied Peter's face curiously. Twice earlier he had heard Peter deny knowing this Jesus they had arrested, but he didn't quite believe him. He decided to test Peter one more time.

He quietly moved out of his place and strolled around the circle, coming up behind the fisherman.

"Didn't I see you with Him in the olive grove?" he probed.

Propelled by fear, Peter's response flew out of his mouth before he could think. "I told you, no!" he fairly shouted.

As the first rays of dawn stole into the courtyard, the rooster crowed. At the sound, Peter's heart sank like a stone. *(Taken from Matthew 26:69-75.)*

HEALING A DIVIDED HEART

From then on, through Jesus' death, Peter hung back in the shadows as God dealt with his divided heart. The chasm between who he longed to be for the Master and who he was slowly narrowed. His broken spirit gained a quiet strength as he faced his weakness, received God's forgiveness and determined what would matter eternally.

By the time of Jesus' resurrection, this fisherman had grown considerably; his fear of men had shrunk to almost nothing. A kingdom not of this world was taking shape in his heart. So when the women brought the news that Jesus had risen from the dead, he ran—without hesitation—to the tomb in belief. And when Jesus personally appeared to him later that very day, the heart with which Peter worshiped his beloved Lord was undivided at last.

MY OWN STRUGGLE

I have seen my own heart reflected in Peter's eyes. I have seen my eagerness to be a fearless follower, but have recognized with pain how easily I have sold truth short when I faced disapproval or rejection. I could be a tower of strength defending the faith from a podium, but a coward to the core when it came to extending the Good News to those who had the ability to make my life miserable if they didn't like what I said.

I have found myself, like Peter in Gethsemane, brandishing a sword after failing to spend the night in prayer, and cowering in a corner when there was no one present to support me.

Furthermore, I have been at times very unsure that what I do in ministry has any value at all, unless someone encourages me. Without the grace of God, I would have bent to every wind. I would have followed the piper who is most enticing and affirming, mistaking charm for wisdom.

FAILING THE TEST

Just ahead of me in the checkout line at the college bookstore stood the most handsome man I had *ever* seen. My heart began to thump and I nearly dropped the stack of textbooks in my arms.

A first-year student from a tiny farming town, I was not in the same league with this guy. But here he was within inches, close enough to reach out and touch. Transfixed, I just stared in awe at this masterpiece, expecting some gorgeous girl to appear at his side at any moment and whisk him away—or at least to the front of the long line.

But no one appeared and to my near-horror, he turned and smiled at me. Sparkling blue eyes which crinkled at the corners as he smiled—topped with curly eyelashes and a suntanned face surrounded by blond curly hair—greeted me. Oblivious to my awestruck stare he began chatting lightly with me. Somehow I found the voice to respond, and by the time we reached the cashier, we had become friends.

He was an English major as well, and heavily involved in drama. Whether the relationship began for him as just another "play" in which to act or not, we found ourselves together a great deal.

He seemed fascinated by my faith and asked many questions at first. But before long he began challenging me, nearly mocking my naiveté for believing, especially, the stories in the Old Testament. In short, in fear of his disapproval—which I simply couldn't bear—I began to compromise. To please him I said that perhaps the Bible might not mean what it says.

But instead of earning his approval, I earned only his scorn. He had been testing me, pressing me in the hope that I would stand strong and true to my beliefs, that *finally* he had found someone who knew God. I failed the test.

In disgust he simply left, dropping out of college to hitchhike aimlessly across the country, leaving behind a letter to me expressing his dejection and saying good-bye. To run from the pain I transferred to a Christian college.

CONFIDENCE BASED ON PRAISE

The kind of confidence that I possessed at that time had come from the effusive praise that my parents had given me while I was growing up; it wasn't deeply grounded in any personal sense of worth in God. Because it was praise-based, all my relationships were destined to be controlled by praise. To ultimately find my confidence in Christ would require a journey though decades of alternating bliss and misery until *who I was* could be determined by *how Christ saw me*. It has taken repeated conscious surrender of worrying about what others think of me and embracing God's sovereignty in my life.

But I can now see the light at the end of the tunnel—and it isn't a train bent on crushing me short of my destination! It is the shadowless presence of the God of peace who has had me under His wing all these years, gently drawing me along toward freedom. His patience has been a marvel.

GOD'S FAITHFULNESS

It is strange, but on the journey I have never doubted God's love for me—even when I failed Him. Perhaps our relationship during those times can be best described by one of the few audible exchanges that I have ever had with the Lord.

After repenting of a grave sin several years ago, I was prostrate on the floor during worship at our church in Lititz, Pennsylvania. Amazingly, at that moment I didn't care in the least what people thought of me. With arms outstretched on the carpet, tears falling, I cried out, "Jesus, please pick me up. Please pick me up!"

To which He gently answered—with a hint of a smile in His voice—"Don't be silly! I never put you down."

He never did put me down. And He never will. He is even praying for me just as He told Peter He would pray for him. He is my best Friend, my Lover, the One who restores my joy and sets the world right side up when I think that all is most lost.

But He's much more than that. He is God. He is holy. He is determined to work the cross through every stronghold and every weakness in my life until I am a rock for Him. He is weaning me from others' approval so that I will depend upon Him alone.

He takes seriously every part of my life, expecting me to repent quickly when I sin and forgive when I am offended. He is the first to lift the load so that I can dance with lightness of heart. He keeps me disciplined and in the traces of obedience and service to the Body of Christ, but *always* He carries the burden for me.

The more I learn of Him, the more childlike I feel and the more content I am to sit at His feet and hear His voice. I am not *afraid* of Him—but I am in *awe* of His majesty and holiness. He is God.

I am His delighted and grateful child—delighted to be held and grateful to be taught by the very Son of God. I am anxious to mature, but never anxious to leave His arms.

QUIET STRENGTH

I love the quiet strength with which Peter later writes his epistles as contained in the New Testament. This Spirit-filled man knows who he is—one of a chosen people, a royal priesthood, a holy nation, a people *belonging* to God. It is because of this grand identity that he—and you and I—can declare the praises of Him who has called us out of darkness into His wonderful light.

As long as we are afraid of what others think of us, as long as our confessions of faith are influenced by the fear of rejection or disapproval or suffering, we will love God out of divided hearts; we will be unstable in all our ways.

Regret will be our companion as we fail to be faithful time after time.

NEW HEARTS

The good news is that a revelation of the love of Jesus Christ and of His suffering for us will do more than mend our miserable hearts—it will give us *new hearts*. The starting point is to ask the Holy Spirit to reveal to us our true condition. Then, as we face our sinfulness squarely and accept God's forgiveness through His Son's heart that was broken for us at Calvary, we see for perhaps the first time how much we are loved.

The light comes on and the understanding that we are fully received in Him is born. We are complete in Him! Furthermore, we are no longer obligated to please a world that is doomed and dying, being strangled by just such sins as we used to hold dear. We can rise to please only Him.

An undivided heart plays a profound role in every generation. The boldness that comes from counting this life as nothing—this life that never gave us any peace for all our trying to please those in it—will enable us to carry the passion of Christ all the way, even to martyrdom, as Peter did.

And if that kind of death comes, we will not think of ourselves as heroes, but as *privileged* to give our lives for Him Who loved us so.

CHAPTER FOUR

DEFEAT OF SHAME

*I sought the LORD, and he answered
me;
he delivered me from all my fears.
Those who look to him are radiant;
their faces are never covered with
shame. (Psalm 34:4-5)*

"For a prophet and messiah, he's sure hard up for good company!" sneered one Pharisee to another. He punctuated his ridicule by spitting into the sand at his feet.

"Remember her?" he asked, pointing a fat, ringed finger at the poorly dressed woman who walked peacefully down the street amidst the little band of common folk who followed Jesus. Her eyes were fixed on His face. "She's probably still mad!" he spoke, loudly enough for her to hear.

"Well, it figures that they travel in the same circles," chimed in his friend. "He casts out demons because he has them himself, they say!" he added disdainfully.

The first man was just getting warmed up to the subject. "And who does she think she is, walking the streets with men in broad daylight!" Again he spat into the sand. "And that man tolerates it, even encourages it! How low can he sink?"

The two men wagged their heads, all the while boldly staring at her.

Mary Magdalene turned just then, and their eyes met. Her gaze was steady and serene, causing both men to quickly turn their heads away. They were suddenly embarrassed to have her see what haunted their own hearts.

She, the delivered, was clean. They, the judges, were befouled by demons of self-righteousness.

Even in their muddled state of mind, they felt strangely undone.

It was a test daily for Mary—especially when young people still laughed at the sight of her just as they had when she had been mad. Their own prowess at mockery so captivated them that they never noticed her sanity. They would have been disappointed to have the game end.

"What a spoilsport Jesus is to have healed me!" she laughed softly.

But it hurt. It hurt when the women whispered behind their hands when she passed by—and grabbed their children to keep them from getting too near. She longed for their company, but it seemed that they could see her only through her past. They couldn't meet the challenge of trusting her now.

Little had changed among those who had known her. But a miracle occurred whenever a man or woman, boy or girl encountered Jesus with a heart broken over sin! Whenever new believers arose forgiven, they claimed her as their own instead of eyeing her suspiciously! It was as though their vision was changed in the instant of repentance, and their hearts set free when forgiven. It was for them just as it had been for her! And how she and they loved one another! *(Taken from Luke 8:1-3.)*

LIVING WITH OUR PASTS

Our pasts are no small thing. Our sins brought hurt and humiliation to those close to us and often made us friends only of the devil himself. Sacred trusts were broken and loved ones withdrew from us to the safety of distance.

But now that we have found Jesus, we are not the same on the inside—this we know. How we wish we could shout the news from the rooftops so everyone else would know it as well! If only we could gather up everyone's old copies of the stories of our pasts so that we could pitch them into a great fire in the town square. If only we could craft new scripts in which there is no remembrance of the mistakes we have made and the evil we have done.

Why does God allow such memories to endure? Wherein is the good for those who are called according to His purpose? If only the memories could be erased.

HAUNTED BY SHAME

Darlene avoided Ted's gaze. She had no right to be spending time with such a great guy. This date was an absolute mistake. *Some things just can't be changed*, she reasoned sadly. No matter how cleaned up she was on the outside, she still felt filthy inside. When men looked at her—even innocently as Ted was now—she cringed, seeing the face of her father leering in her memory in the semidarkness of her bedroom. As hard as she tried to erase it, this scene invaded every encounter she had with a man.

It was her fault that he had abused her, her father had told her over and over. It was she who had betrayed her mother. The old accusations rushed over her spirit. She was evil and dirty, just as he had said she was. An involuntary shudder ran through her body.

"Are you cold?" Ted asked with concern, quickly taking off his jacket and gently placing it around her shoulders as they stood side by side on the ocean boardwalk that cool spring evening.

She tried to protest, but he insisted. "I can't let you freeze, you know," he said teasingly. "Besides, the jacket looks better on you than on me anyway," he pronounced with a smile.

She could still feel the warmth from his body on the inside of the jacket. Longing to enjoy its coziness, she tried desperately to resist the thought that she was only defiling him by touching it.

How could she ever have a relationship with such a decent guy? Even though she was now a Christian trying to make a fresh start, shame repeatedly threatened to overwhelm her from the inside out.

Does Jesus really love me enough to take my place on the cross? she wondered as she stared at the sunset. *Will He somehow bring to an end these feelings of unworthiness?* She tentatively pulled the coat comfortingly around her and, with that act of faith, shame began to lose its power.

OUR PAIN

When we have been abused, especially sexually, defilement seems to cling to us like rotting grave clothes. Our very nerve endings vibrate dissonantly from the effects of shameful deeds done by and to us—our peace and security in the goodness of life have been systematically destroyed by each offense.

Our hearts are in ashes and we wish we could die—but our senses betray us and we feel on. Every encounter with those "who know" jolts our sensibilities and sends pain waves along raw nerves. Our heads drop and we wish to disappear, feeling worthless and irredeemable. All but the most common functions of life seem overwhelming. Our identities have been stolen.

JESUS AND SHAME

Jesus too experienced shame—but it didn't make Him shameful. Why not? Because it didn't come from the inside. He didn't "own" it for Himself as we do, for He had no part in the deeds which gave birth to the shame. His suffering was for our sake.

However, in others' eyes the shame was just as real upon Him as that which heaps itself upon us. Because of His disgrace nearly everyone abandoned Him. They ran from Him, horrified by the spectacle He created when stripped and beaten beyond recognition. They deserted Him when the sky turned inky black and the ground shook. They found no place in their hearts to wonder if the accusations were even true. It was their nature to believe the worst.

Somehow, despising Him made them feel a little taller than before. His weakness made them feel strong. For a moment they could think themselves quite righteous; one-upping God has always been the name of the game.

SHAME NEVER OWNED

He *knew* shame fully—all the shame of the world, past, present and future (for He has never been trapped in linear time as are we)—and the image of shame repulsed His generation. But He never *owned* the shame. He accepted it and didn't deny it, but He knew that when He rose again—after having placed His spirit in the hands of the Father at death—the shame would have no power over Him again.

People could think what they wanted to about Him through the centuries; He would love them until their hearts broke in response. He would be a King for us regardless of how little others might expect of Him. The shame from before the resurrection could not stick to Him afterward. He would reign regardless.

Man's opinions could only wound *them*, could only retard *their* maturity, could only bind *them*. He was free inside, receiving His identity only through His role as the Son of God.

JESUS TAKES OUR SHAME

And so it must be with us. When we die with Him, willing to let the past be judged by Him alone, *the shame is transferred to Him.* His tender mercy carefully plucks it from our hearts and binds it to the cross—away from us *forever* in the eyes of God. We don't "own" it anymore. We are God's own sons and daughters, heirs with Jesus to His throne: that is our identity. We will reign with Him regardless of the past—or of what people think of us.

THOSE WHO JUDGE

The condition of those who judge us is sad. Those who have never fully embraced their own sinfulness and taken it humbly to the cross still have "old eyes." They see through the screen of their own clouded and begrudging states and misinterpret the facts altogether. They have physical eyes, but they seem blind to the miracle of cleansing that has occurred in our lives. They *can't* see our cleanness, not because we are still dirty, but because their lenses are. It is not our job to try to change their vision. We can't do it. They are only treating us as men of old treated Jesus—so we are in good company. Jesus didn't defend His own purity. He knew truth would stand in the end.

But we can pray for them. We can love and forgive them just as Jesus did, for "they do not know what they are doing" (Luke 23:34). Besides, we once, like them, desperately needed grace.

LIFE REDEEMED

While we can remember our shame, it no longer lives inside. In the remembering is much blessing, for it keeps us tender and grateful. It prevents us from binding shame about the neck of the next man. Best of all, our love for Jesus grows deeper daily because of the shame we wish to forget and can't. We who have been healed of so much pain through His great love, love that much more.

Jesus's sacrifice on the cross for our shame not only redeems life, it turns into jewels the ashes of the past. Shame on the inside is dead, and we have been raised to newness of life—no matter what others may say.

In that newness we will walk—not with our noses in the air—but with our eyes fixed on Jesus, Who has set us free. And when Satan tries to accuse us again, the Holy Spirit will hold us fast. Only affirmation will shine from our Savior's eyes as He lovingly returns our gaze.

CHAPTER FIVE

BIRTH OF GRACE

Humble yourselves before the Lord,
and he will lift you up. (James 4:10)

The insistent sputtering of the oil lamp finally won his attention. Paul rose from his study desk, rummaged in the cupboard for more oil and carefully refilled the lamp's reservoir.

After trimming the wick and relighting it, the stocky, angular-featured man settled down once again to his studies, his bushy eyebrows knit in concentration. He could hear the family in the rooms below preparing for breakfast and a new day.

How strange it all seemed. Here he was, back in Tarsus where he had begun—starting all over again.

When he had left here as a lad to study under Gamaliel in Jerusalem some twenty-four years before, he had been so sure of everything. His had been a life of books and facts, the Jewish laws and contempt for anything that smacked of heresy against them. His world had been painted in two colors—black and white. All else was frivolity.

Suddenly his hands shook as he remembered another color that had dominated his days only a few short years ago. Waves of red washed over the room as he recalled the blood of a young follower of "The Way" named Stephen. He, then called Saul, had helped kill Stephen by assent in a fever pitch of hatred.

There had been others—stoned to death or imprisoned until being assigned death at a later time. Such memories now tore at his heart.

But the blood that haunted him the most—yet supernaturally bathed him in consolation—was the blood of a man named Jesus, the Messiah, the very Son of God—whom his revered teachers of the law had destroyed and taught the young zealot to hate!

By the convicting power of the Holy Spirit and through a blinding encounter with the risen Jesus, his mind had been changed forever and his heart made new. Once his towering intellect had been his ballast in the storm of controversy. Now his heart—won by the love and compassion of the Lord Jesus Christ—was fearlessly on fire to share the news of salvation to all who would listen. He the persecutor was now the believer.

His was a life turned upside down.

He brushed his now-steady hands over his face to clear the images from his eyes. Paul hesitated, then put down his pen and rose to stretch. He had been in prayer and study all night long, sorting out issues from the Law and finding them fulfilled in Christ. It was amazing!

Pulling his robe tighter about himself in anticipation of the chilly morning air, he threw open the shutters and looked into the streets below. Gentile merchants were already setting up their wares, getting ready for another brisk day of trade. Lifting his eyes to the horizon, he could see in the harbor the masts of ships laden with goods from all over the world. They seemed to beckon him to distant lands where Jesus was not yet known.

"I must tell them," he murmured. He watched the faces of the men and women below in the streets and imagined those he would see during his journeys in the years ahead. His heart ached for them all in a way still new to this previously cold and calculating legalist.

The love of God had changed his life. He would risk everything to tell them of the Savior who had died for them. The security of the past—position and prestige as one of the Jewish religious elite—was a dim memory for which he did not mourn.

His life was now consumed by the Christ who had set him free from the law of sin and death. And for this Christ he would willingly die. *(Taken from Acts 7:54-8:1; 9:1-31.)*

LAW YIELDS TO GRACE

Saul had always been a perfectionist—a man driven to make the world right by his own high standards, a man who drove himself to meet those same standards. There was no in-between for him, no tolerable mediocrity. As a Pharisee, this trait had made him a tyrant who acted as though mercy were weakness.

The kind of perfection he sought before becoming a believer in Christ was easy to legislate. It could be achieved by fierce self-discipline and adherence to the pages of the Law—which were flat and two-dimensional. The Law provided a convenient mental steel trap and asked nothing of the spirit or the heart of a man. Love was particularly difficult for a perfectionist, because it required a release of expectations and a greatness of trust. So it never entered the picture.

But then this Christ died for just such men who hated Him! He loved them, and that love begged a response. It had taken a blinding experience to awaken Saul's heart and persuade his mind. He had no longer been able to tell what truth was and was not; he could not see. He had to listen with his spirit for perhaps the first time in his life.

During his three days without eyesight, God convicted Saul's heart. His power to control others—and even his own destiny—was gone. He was at God's mercy, and God was there for him.

When he allowed the very people he had sought to kill to pray for him, his sight returned and he was filled with the Holy Spirit. What a turnabout!

The way to deliverance for many of us who demand perfection of ourselves and others is often to be humbled before those we respect least. That is God's mercy. It may be the only way to get us to understand forgiveness.

As we discover that grace and mercy come quickly and gently from God when we sin, we begin to learn how to extend that same grace and mercy to others. They, like us, are flawed and in much need of help to see the love and power of God. They, like us, will be won by mercy, not by Law.

Pride in Perfection

Mr. Cooper was never wrong. That's the message he gave his sons and his daughter from the earliest days of their lives. That's the image he projected to everyone he knew. If it appeared to others that he might have made a mistake, woe unto the one who dared tell him so.

Mr. Cooper was a good man by many standards. He worked hard to support his family, carefully researched ways to improve his huge poultry ranch and took his family to church faithfully. He even surprised folks on occasion by his generosity in hard times.

But his family had a secret. Behind closed doors Mr. Cooper was an impossible man to please. Being good enough was always just out of reach. And when one of his children failed to meet his high expectations, the harsh lectures and the days of cold silence that followed were worse than a thousand whippings.

There were rules—lots of rules—about how to dress, how to act, how to look and how to believe. They were, as Mr. Cooper was quick to point out, "to keep these kids from bringing disgrace upon God's name and ruining our reputation."

Trying to Measure Up

Hannah suffered the most as they were growing up. As the only girl among five children, she was expected to carry a heavy load of household chores. She was to help her mother keep things in order, according to the standards set by Mr. Cooper. Mrs. Cooper had no time to play with Hannah; everyone had a multitude of tasks each day to keep the family business running smoothly.

Hannah saw her dad only at suppertime when he was tired and grouchy. But he was never too exhausted to sternly question her on her schoolwork and how helpful she might have been that day. Six o'clock in the evening—as soon as the food had been passed and their plates were full—was quiz time. Seldom could she digest that meal well, for her stomach churned until it was over. Then he moved from the table to his armchair to read from his many trade journals. She sensed that whatever she answered would not show sufficient intelligence or responsibility to suit him.

Her mother always tried to sing a little as they cleared away the dishes, attempting to lighten Hannah's heaviness. But they never talked. Hannah ached to confide in her mom about her hopes, fears and dreams. Her mother was always too busy or too tired to sit with her and help her open up. In this family each lived in a private little world of his or her own. Only trying to please Mr. Cooper bound them together.

LONGING FOR APPROVAL

How she wished her father would hug her or play fun games with her and her brothers like other fathers did. She wondered what that would be like. *The boys have to work hard too, but at least they have Dad with them*, she thought a bit jealously. Maybe they even laughed once in a while out there in the barn—they never said. But daily, as Hannah moved from grade school to high school, she longed for her father's affection.

"Am I pretty?" Hannah asked her mirror the day she turned fourteen. "I wonder if any man will ever tell me that I am." She combed her long, wavy brown hair and then pulled it into a ponytail with a soft yellow ribbon.

"Are all men as stern and demanding as Daddy?" she asked the mirror again. Then heaving a sigh, she laid her hairbrush down and turned to leave for school.

There was a new boy that day at school, a little old for their grade. She heard that it was because his family had moved around a lot, and he had fallen behind.

He was nice—especially to Hannah. Robbie noticed the yellow ribbon in her hair right away. When he saw her looking at him, he quickly broke into a broad grin and said, "Hannah, you sure are pretty."

She was embarrassed at his attention at first. But day after day, she found herself fixing her hair to please him. She did whatever she could to draw the sweet compliments from him that he seemed only too happy to give. At night she lay in bed replaying them, savoring every word and gesture.

After school one afternoon Robbie caught up with her in the hallway. With a new look in his eyes that made her heart skip a beat, he said into her ear, "There's no one like you, Hannah. You are so special." He put his arms around her waist and gave her a big hug.

Hannah was speechless and turned red immediately, which made Robbie smile. She loved his touch, and he knew it. He had never seen a girl so hungry for affection.

"I've got my dad's car today, Hannah. Let me drive you home," he said persuasively. "Your brothers are all at the soccer game and will never know the difference." Remembering that her father would be the real problem, he added, "I'll drop you off at your bus stop, and your folks won't suspect a thing. OK?"

Within three months, Hannah was pregnant. Soon after, Robbie's family moved again, leaving Hannah to face her father alone. But she couldn't do it. She ran away instead.

Before long, everyone knew what had happened, and besides being desperately worried about Hannah, Mr. Cooper was humiliated. His perfect family had fallen apart. He had failed, and he couldn't forgive himself—or Hannah.

CONVICTION FALLS

Late one night Mr. Cooper broke under the strain. Alone in the hayloft in the dimly lit barn, he fell on his face and begged God to help him go on.

As the fire of the Holy Spirit revealed to him how his pride and his rules had driven Hannah to someone else for love, he wept in pain and repentance. Gradually the tears subsided as he felt the forgiveness of God work its way through his soul.

Suddenly he saw Hannah, as a little girl, pleading with him to play with her.

"God, give me another chance. Please bring her back so that I can tell her that I love her," he pleaded.

Early the next morning, just as he was leaving for the barn to begin his chores, the phone rang. It was Hannah. She wanted to come home.

JESUS DIED FOR OUR FAILURES

Our expectations of ourselves and others to meet impossible standards must go to the cross. They can't be met. And when we fail and insist upon clinging to the deep sense of failure that washes over us, we grieve God and wound those we love. His Son died for that failure; it doesn't surprise Him. He will make short work of it if we will repent of the pride of trying to save ourselves.

He loves us so much that He wants to free us from the horrid cycle of blame and self-recrimination that we go through whenever we make the slightest mistake. He wants to teach us to separate others' failures from who they are inside, so that our relationships are not destroyed and we can learn to love unconditionally. God allows our own sowing and reaping to humble us—and then is there to pick us up. He encourages us to become as little children and to start over with ourselves and with others.

To have a mind fully persuaded for Christ and His cross, the reduction must happen. Life must become simplified and our hearts taken back to the place of childlike trust. Love must replace Law.

By letting the cross, through repentance, put to death all our unrealistic expectations of perfection, our deliverance begins. As we repent of playing God over our lives and others' (and of believing that we actually are *capable* of perfection), Jesus takes the terrible burden and receives us as we are. Life becomes a gentle pleasure and our loneliness is gone.

Jesus is in love with us, and He has given His life to set us free. The cross will kill the sins within us and make us faithful, merciful servants. We will find that the rules of love are blissfully few.

CHECKING OURSELVES

Reading the signals within our circumstances is critical. God is moving through them. For perfectionists, failure is usually the blessed key step to humility and release from impossible expectations. Failure also puts us among friends. Not one of us is perfect.

Let's listen with our spirits first, rather than our minds. Let's refuse to try to heal ourselves during failure by building higher walls and sterner expectations. Besides, His love can penetrate any barrier. The sooner we surrender, the sooner we will be free.

Perfection can turn, as it did for Paul, into the passion of selfless excellence. That excellence comes from relying on God's power in our lives and forsaking our own.

Such passion is found at the cross.

As we arise forgiven and free, the very trait that had previously driven us to destruction makes us men and women of perseverance, faithfulness and deep integrity.

FULLY RECEIVED AND FORGIVEN

He who *is* perfect refuses to condemn us when we make mistakes and repent. Then who are we to hold our sins against ourselves? By humbly identifying with Him who is truly perfect, we are made whole. As we take our sins to the cross, Jesus covers us with His death. The blood of the Lamb washes us clean.

When we know in our hearts and minds that He fully receives us—failures and all—and loves us unconditionally, then forgiveness and loving acceptance to others will flow.

And life becomes a joy.

CHAPTER SIX

REST IN HIM

He who dwells in the shelter of the
Most High
will rest in the shadow of the
Almighty.
I will say of the LORD, *"He is my*
refuge and my fortress,
my God, in whom I trust."
(Psalm 91:1-2)

There was no sleep that night. Her mind, spent from the day's cosmic calamity, drifted beyond her control. From the past to the present and back again it freely wandered as she lay in bed in John's home, where she would live from now on.

Closing her eyes, Mary could hear her own voice singing the melody which the Holy Spirit had given her thirty-four years ago. It came only days after the angel had told her she would bear the Son of God.

> My soul glorifies the Lord
>   and my spirit rejoices in God my
>   Savior,
> for he has been mindful
>   of the humble state of his servant.
> From now on all generations will call
>   me blessed,
>   for the Mighty One has done great
>   things for me—
>   holy is his name.
> His mercy extends to those who fear
>   him,
>   from generation to generation.
> He has performed mighty deeds with
>   his arm;
>   he has scattered those who are proud
>   in their inmost thoughts.

He has brought down rulers from their
      thrones
  but has lifted up the humble.
He has filled the hungry with good
      things
  but has sent the rich away empty.
He has helped his servant Israel,
  remembering to be merciful
to Abraham and his descendants
      forever,
  even as he said to our fathers.
(Luke 1:46-55)

As she pulled the covers close, trying to recapture that day long ago, Mary whispered in wonder into the dark room, "How true the song was after all! Jesus *did* all that He promised to do, didn't He?" Remembering His gentle but firm voice, she was comforted.

LOOKING BACK

Then her mind traveled back to the days of His youth when He had stayed behind in Jerusalem without telling her and Joseph. They had been worried sick when He turned up missing! He had expected her to know, to understand that He had come of age and was no longer her child in the same way as in years past. The higher call had demanded a response, and He had answered. His identity had been established that day, and He had expected her to understand.

She remembered how, only a few short years ago, He had read a segment of Isaiah in the synagogue in Nazareth:

> "The Spirit of the Lord is on me,
>> because He has anointed me
>> to preach good news to the poor.
> He has sent me to proclaim freedom
>> for the prisoners
>> and recovery of sight for the blind,
> to release the oppressed,
>> to proclaim the year of the Lord's
>> favor." (Luke 4:18-19)

She smiled in spite of her sorrow, saying softly, "He read to them about Himself!" It still amazed her.

And then there was that first miracle at the wedding in Cana. She had urged Him to act because she *knew* that He truly *could* turn the water into wine. A smile touched her lips again as she thought, *We were a team that day*. But her face saddened a bit as she remembered how He had moved on without needing her prompting after that. He loved her, but expected her—now even more than before—to understand that He was no longer of this earth. It had been hard, but she had let Him go.

Those early days had been easy. Miracles, applause, repentance, changed lives and joy in anticipating the kingdom that had come to earth. But clouds had hung above them even in the good times. The murmuring of the Jewish leaders had cast a tense backdrop to the drama created by the

Good News that set the captives free. If the Pharisees had hated her, she wouldn't have minded. She was sinful just as anyone. But that they hated Jesus, the very Son of God, made chills of dread run through her slender frame.

"What will become of them?" she spoke into the night.

Her thoughts jumped without warning to His infancy—to the days when His tiny fingers had clutched strands of her hair that had fallen within His reach as she rocked Him to sleep.

How she loved Him! How hard it had been not to react in anger every time He was misunderstood and spoken against! It had been all she could do to entrust Him into His Father's care, even though she knew it all must be.

Beyond Her Control

Life had been full of ups and downs. Dreams born, then surrendered. Hope renewed at the sound of hosannas just one week ago, then murder upon the cross this very day. And now the silence of the grave.

What had old Simeon prophesied thirty-three years ago when she and Joseph had taken Jesus to the temple to be dedicated?

> This child is destined to cause the falling and rising of many in Israel, and to be a sign that will be spoken against, so that the thoughts of many hearts will be revealed. (2:34-35)

"And a sword will pierce your own soul too," he had said after blessing the child (2:35, emphasis added). How true that had been!

God's plan for His life had always been beyond her control; it had never crossed her mind to refuse that plan. Through all the agony and loss, hopes and fears, He had indisputably been God come to earth. There could have been no other way. She had surrendered the desire to snatch Jesus away from danger and hurry Him into hiding time after time.

Now the pall of death that had descended upon all the believers in Jerusalem, stretching to envelop those in every town Jesus had visited, begged a response from God. She knew, even while she wept at His death, that the response would come. *(Taken from John 19:25-27.)*

LEARNING TO TRUST

What kept Mary from losing her mind—and her faith—when her son hung dead upon the cross? What kept her from cursing God for letting her child suffer such pain, abuse and horror at the hands of those He had sought to save?

What holds us fast when our children suffer rejection or debilitating illness—even death? What keeps *us* from losing our minds—or our faith—in the midst of family crises?

MY OWN BATTLE

I remember when our own daughter, at six months, was suffering from relapse after relapse of silent croup. With no warning, in the middle of the night, she could barely breathe. She couldn't call out, so I spent every night at her bedroom door where I would be able to hear her strain for air in time to rush her to the hospital. During those nights, intense fear gripped my heart. I feared that if I dozed off for a second, I would lose her. Her life seemed to depend upon me, my vigilance, my control over circumstances. Most frightening was that I knew it was beyond me. I couldn't save her even if I monitored her every breath. It was the greatest horror I had ever encountered. I was helpless.

I fought another wrestling match as well—with God. Could I trust Him with her life? Did I think I loved her more than He did? Was I convinced, as I had always told others, that He was a *good* God?

If I let go, would He let her die?

Letting Go

Finally, weeping as I knelt at the couch outside her bedroom door, I held my hands out in front of me. In one last enormous struggle, I let Julie go. I gave her to Him.

It was settled in my heart once and for all: God is good, and His ways are good. He loves both my children more than I could ever hope to. He will be good to them, and He will be good to me. I realized that night that Julie had belonged to Him long before she came to me; I was simply giving her back. In fact, without God's love I wouldn't have had her at all, for He is the Life-giver. And He knows best how to take her home.

Although Julie's illness was far from over, I slept peacefully. I *knew* at last that God would wake me if He needed me. I could trust Him.

SURRENDER BRINGS INTIMACY

Six months later, God healed Julie instantaneously after the Holy Spirit had spoken to my heart that she would be. But He could have decided differently and would not have been any less loving or trustworthy.

I see now that the most critical element of that experience was surrendering my children to God. This led me into a new dimension of intimacy with Him. It was essential for me, and for my children's spiritual health, that I resolve how I saw God's love. Something happened that night. It was as though earth receded and heaven became home. It had suddenly seemed very miserly of me to plead that Julie remain on this miserable little planet if God wanted her to be with Him. I could not be so selfish.

I had been weeping for me, not her. I had been counting on her life for my joy. Without her I had thought I'd die. But when I fixed my eyes on Jesus and stretched to see heaven, I was convinced that whatever my Father decided would be good.

REST IN HIM

We will experience death triumphantly when we first come to grips with life, which has been given us by the love of God. It becomes a solid fact: Heaven and earth are His. Yielding our lives to Him brings another solid fact: He *has taken* those lives. We no longer live to ourselves. We no longer belong to ourselves. We and all we have are His.

If we hold back any part of ourselves—such as our children or spouse—we will be torn apart. With one foot in the kingdom of earth and one in the kingdom of heaven, we become dismembered. This pain—and its deadening effect upon our spirits—is not worth the hollow sense of ownership to which we cling.

There will be no peace, only fear, until we trust Him. Until then, because of the time we spend listening to the enemy's lies, we wonder if God is cruel and sadistic. A twisted and distorted image of God brings horror to our dreams as we fight to keep what long ago we said was His.

But when we give our loved ones to Him in earnest trust—even amid the fear of loss—His sovereignty in our lives is established. Our fragmentation ends, our turmoil stills. The icy fingers of dread withdraw from our hearts and we see His loving face again.

Heaven comes back into focus and our brief time here on earth regains its goal: that we grow into His likeness. This always requires surrender to a plan with more eternal significance than the brief earthly good that we clutch.

PROBING QUESTIONS

Do we trust God? Do we believe that He loves us far beyond our wildest dreams? Will we rest in Him and say "yes" to whatever cross He may ask us to die upon, even when we don't understand why? Can we say as did Mary, "May it be to me as you have said" (Luke 1:38)?

CHAPTER SEVEN

RESTORATION

For you were like sheep going astray, but now you have returned to the Shepherd and Overseer of your souls. (1 Peter 2:25)

"Any news, Micah? Has anyone seen my son?" Enan anxiously questioned the messenger as he offered the young man a cool drink of water from the well in front of the beautiful family home.

Micah wiped the sweat from his forehead with the linen towel his host had handed him and slowly drank the water. He tried to think how best to answer this man whose son had left home with his inheritance and come to ruin in a distant country. The news was not good.

"I'm afraid that whatever you gave him is gone," the messenger began, avoiding the father's eyes.

"I don't care about the money," Enan responded softly, searching Micah's face for more information. "I just want to know if he is all right."

"He's alive, sir, and far from the city and the mess he got into there."

Enan pressed him further. "But where is he now? Do you know?" Worry filled his words.

Micah handed him the empty cup and continued. "He's working for a pig farmer just outside Israel's borders," he began cautiously. Micah decided not to tell Enan about how thin and weak the boy had become nor how desperately lonely he was.

Micah tried to smile as he quickly changed the subject.

"And how's your other son, Enan?" he asked.

"Oh, faithful to his work," he responded thoughtfully. "But it's never been easy to get close to him. I love him just as much," Enan added sincerely. "I just wish he understood my heart a little bit better." He felt awkward talking about such things.

"How I miss Zuri," he added with a sigh.

A DREAM FULFILLED

Daily Enan's eyes scanned the horizon for signs of his younger son's return. His heart told him that Zuri would come back someday. The bond between them, though stretched thin by distance, was still strong.

And then late one chilly winter's afternoon—just as the sun was about to slip behind the western mountains—a lone and limping figure stumbled into the southern pasture. The cattle shifted uneasily to give him room to pass, not recognizing the tattered, barefoot vagabond.

The stirring caught Enan's attention as he fed the horses behind the barn. His muscles tensed, and he instinctively reached for a stout stick to fend off whatever was disturbing the animals.

As he secured the corral gate and started toward the pasture, who should emerge from among the cattle but his son, Zuri! The father let out a cry as he recognized the outline headed his way. Dropping the stick, he ran to reach his weary, homesick child.

As Enan wrapped his loving arms around the boy, Zuri's legs gave out. He fell to the ground weeping. Enan dropped the ground with him, drawing Zuri's head to rest upon his own chest. He gently stroked the boy's tangled, dirty hair.

Zuri once again heard the beating of his father's heart. Memories of childhood surged over him and caused him—however weakly—to laugh and cry at the same time. The steady heartbeat spoke of the patience, the suffering, the tenderness, the purposeful discipline that had come from this man who would gladly give his life for either of his sons.

Zuri knew in that moment that he had come *home*—not only to his father, but also to himself. Missing that heartbeat had brought him back. In its absence, he had nearly lost his own soul. Now he knew he would never leave home again. *(Taken from Luke 15:11-32.)*

OUR SELFISHNESS

How often do we "leave home?" How often do we forget the Father's heartbeat and move to the pulse of the world, the flesh and the devil? How many times have we been interested only in our Father's fortune and begged for our inheritance early—for life to be easy, painless and without sacrifice *now*? How often has our devotion to God depended upon answers to our prayers that suit us, rather than those that make us grow up?

While God's blessings and deliverance are wonderful gifts—often coming when we least expect them—most of us do not handle constant ease well. Comfort entices us to leave His presence. When comfort becomes the mainstay of our happiness, we become devoted to sustaining it rather than to seeking intimacy with the One who loves us.

Furthermore, when our lives are "golden," we lose touch with those who suffer around us. We grow aloof from misery, thinking it an inconvenience and a mark of lesser beings than ourselves. We begin to judge others and expect them to arrive at success by the formula we think helped us get there. We become impatient with their stumbling. We forget that we are all each other's keeper, and we leave them along the side of the road.

Compassion dies when we have no pain like theirs. Jesus felt the pain we feel at the devil's onslaught; therefore His compassion is genuine. He understands our temptations, but He knows that understanding is not enough. There must be victory.

CHANGED HEARTS

In bringing us the victory, God does not remove us from the world. He doesn't change our social status, race, education, gender, income or appearance. *He changes our hearts.* As we learn to love Him and listen to Him, He cleanses and renews our minds, helps us surrender our wills to His and heals our damaged emotions. He transforms us from the inside out.

Daily life, however, may not become easier.

FACING THE MUSIC

The heavy gray thunderheads lumbered across the sky as white clouds scurried out of their way.

Marcus glanced at them as he walked unsteadily down a side street in the "Windy City."

"Great," he muttered. "All I need is to get soaked in another storm."

"There's always the bar on Seventh Street," a sinister voice whispered into his subconscious. Marcus turned to follow the voice as he had a million times before, but the thought of another drink suddenly made him nauseous. His head ached, and the garbage cans, storefronts and battered parking meters swirled in confusion before his glazed eyes. He sank to the pavement and passed out.

Remembering Home

He began to dream. It was nighttime at home. In a two-bedroom bungalow in a little town in Western Pennsylvania slept his wife of seven years. In his dream he could see Jenny lying there alone. The pillow next to hers, where he had once laid his head, was empty. He was sure he heard her sigh in her sleep.

In the second bedroom slept Heather, his little girl, tucked in beneath a flowered comforter. He remembered every detail in her room, right down to the doll perched on a small chair next to her dresser. As he dreamed of her, his heart ached with nearly unbearable pain.

The pain woke him just as the rain began, the wind whipping bits of trash and old newspapers into his face. God had saved and delivered him from the streets years ago, before he met Jenny. Now was he really returning to the gutter from which he came? Could anger at others have again the power to destroy his life? His heart pounded as a new resolve formed in his mind.

I'm going home! I've had enough of this! Marcus set his jaw in determination. He pulled himself to his feet and bent into the wind, heading for the bus station. He would panhandle enough money for the ticket and go home.

God! he cried out in his heart, *Take me back! Forgive me for my bitterness toward my boss for firing me. Forgive me for my bitterness toward the church. Forgive me for running away from my family. I am so sorry!* Wiping the rain from his eyes he whispered, "Just take me home."

TAKEN BACK TO REBUILD

God took Marcus home—to Himself and to the little town that he had left two years earlier.

Marcus began to learn of the cross. He learned that only Jesus could bear the weight of others' willful—or unintentional—sins against him. Carrying anger and revenge had only eaten away at Marcus' life and caused pain for his loved ones. He had to forgive. As he repented and fixed his eyes on Jesus, peace returned.

But Jenny was not happy to see him. Memories of his anger, abandonment, betrayal and the subsequent financial struggle were too fresh to be brushed aside. She needed to learn to trust him again. Perhaps she would never be able to let him into her heart. She protected herself by keeping Marcus at arm's length.

Because Jenny wouldn't let him move back in, he submitted himself to a Christian residential discipleship program. There, as he wept over his losses, he learned many lessons.

He discovered that there is a price to be paid for sin. Yes, Jesus' blood breaks the curse upon us and forgiveness flows from heaven. Spiritually, He suspends the law of sowing and reaping. However, it often still impacts relationships in this life.

Marcus could not demand that others see him as God saw him. Having sown desertion and unforgiveness, he would reap a harvest of separation and suspicion—no matter how much he tried to convince his family that he had changed. He had to place Jenny and Heather in God's hands and let go.

RELEASING OTHERS

Those we wound cannot be automatically healed by our decisions—no matter how redemptive. Each person must find the Healer individually. We may never be able to convince our loved ones that we are now trustworthy. If we were unfaithful before, why should they trust us now?

We must understand how empty our promises sound and forgive their hesitation. After all, we damaged their ability to trust.

UNDERSTANDING THE CROSS

While we are under conviction for our sins, just as the thief who hung alongside Jesus, there is a split second when we gain revelation. There we are—guilty through and through, pain shooting along every nerve, alienated from earth and all who are on it. The grave is our just desert. Then we feel the eyes of Jesus upon us. As our eyes meet His, life as we had fashioned it falls from our hands and our hearts cease beating in self-defense. His grace invades our lives, and a new man in Christ is born. Joy returns—not as the world gives, but as His presence guarantees.

As we surrender our claim to being lord of our destinies and judge of all, His life moves into ours. A new heart beats within us; we begin seeing life—and sin—as He does. Our desire becomes to do only His will. Our spirits become led by the Spirit of Christ. Like the thief on the cross, He takes us to paradise, where God rules.

And like Marcus, when we come back from the death of sin, we may have nothing left in the world, but we will be free. We may be without friends and kin, but the God of heaven has promised never to leave us nor forsake us. Our failures may have forever altered our future, but His Spirit will begin opening doors to minister as never before.

THOSE WE HAVE HURT

Is there hope for reconciliation for Marcus and Jenny? Can broken marriages and relationships be mended? Can abandoned, betrayed people trust again?

After betrayal, walls of self-protection go up around wounded hearts. They thicken daily, depending upon the duration and degree of the offenses. Coping mechanisms snap into place. Strength is found to shape a new life without the betrayer. But beneath the facade of control surge anger, disappointment, regret and fear. Bitterness fights to rule the day.

Yes, reconciliation is possible. But only if the injured are willing to yield to the Holy Spirit. To forgive and release the bitterness will take a monumental death to self-protection. The willingness to be vulnerable will take a divine encounter and identification with Jesus who, more innocent than they could ever be, was likewise betrayed.

By His Grace

Only the love of God can enable us to love the ones who hurt us. If we pin all our hopes on them again, we will be on dangerous ground. Our peace and fulfillment do not depend on other people. They do not have the ability to be that perfect. It is a mistake to draw our strength and affirmation from a human heartbeat, for that heartbeat can possibly fail once more. Only the Father's heartbeat remains constant. Only with our heads on His chest will we be comforted, restored and secure in the future. Only there will we grow in our ability to love unconditionally.

Jenny's ability to try again will not come when Marcus proves that he has changed—although that will play a part. It will come from her own willingness to release vengeance and deepen her identification with Christ. She will have her own cross to embrace. As memories resurface and Marcus inevitably does and says things that remind her of past pain, she will need to exercise forgiveness again and again.

The relationship may never be as it was before, but it can be vastly richer because of the intentional self-surrender both make day by day. It will lead to loving one another by choice, valuing one another as God does—an unselfish honoring. Restored trust will not come quickly; it may take a lifetime. But by grace it is possible.

CHANGED IN HIS PRESENCE

It was midnight when she finally turned off her bedside lamp and laid her Bible aside. It was still open to Matthew 6:14, "For if you forgive men when they sin against you, your heavenly Father will also forgive you." Jenny wrapped her arms around her pillow and slid under the covers. Tears rolled down her cheeks as she prayed.

"God, I know that You have forgiven Marcus and given him a fresh start. When he calls on the phone, I can hear the love in his voice. I know that he hopes for another chance."

She reached for a tissue on the bedside stand.

"I think I have forgiven him," she continued. "At least I have tried. I don't sense the ache in the pit of my stomach anymore. But I don't feel love either. It's gone. If I let him come back, what emotion can I give him so that the bitterness will not return?"

Out of the stillness, Jesus spoke to her spirit. "Jenny, can you feel My compassion for him, the compassion that took me to Calvary for you both even before you called out My name? I will teach you how to see him as I do. Take your time, Jenny. Learn of Me and go with Me to the cross."

Jenny sat up suddenly and snapped the light back on. She grabbed her Bible and began to read hungrily. As she opened her heart that night, compassion slowly filled the empty places as Jesus poured His heart into hers.

Hope Restored

It was a supernatural transaction. Through the months and years of pain and separation, Jenny had learned to hear the Father's heartbeat. He had prepared her for this very moment. With His compassion filling her life, she had something new to give to Marcus. Perhaps in time it would turn to love. As Jenny fell asleep that night, the seeds of restoration—sown in her tender heart by the God who loved her—began to grow.

PART 2:

SHADOWS OF
RESISTANCE

CHAPTER EIGHT

UNWILLINGNESS TO REPENT

See to it that no one misses the grace of God and that no bitter root grows up to cause trouble and defile many. (Hebrews 12:15)

With his offering of vegetables wilting in the sun—unaccepted by God and now looking foolish even to Cain—his fingers curled into fists. The more he saw his own humiliation, the more intense became his anger. God's voice surrounded him, urging him to take warning.

"Why are you angry? Why is your face downcast?" the Lord probed Cain's heart with gentle persistence. "If you do what is right, will you not be accepted?"

Cain's fist tightened. "So now I am to be reprimanded like a child?" he seethed through clenched teeth. "I, the elder, am made to look like a fool!"

His brother Abel, bowed in worship nearby, was unaware of the anger surging through Cain's body. But after he had seen the sacrifice that Cain had placed upon the altar, he had feared for his brother. They both knew better. They had been taught since childhood that blood must be shed for sin. As beautiful as Cain's vegetables were, they would never do.

Cain wrestled with his pride, refusing to own his error and set it right. Then the Lord's voice cut across his mind with words of dire warning. "But if you do not do what is right, sin is crouching at your door! It desires to have you, but you must master it!"

In a single instant he would decide: surrender or rebellion. It was that simple. The former would involve his own pain; the latter would multiply pain into generations to come.

To rally anger to ward off the conviction of God's words, Cain focused upon Abel. It seemed that Abel was always showing him up. Wasn't he, Cain, good enough for God?

"Well, Abel's not good enough for *me*!" he spit out the words as he tossed his rejected offering into the bushes.

Cain had made the choice. Revenge consumed the energy that could have gone into repenting. A few hours later in a field not far from the altar, Cain attacked and murdered his brother! As the blood ran into the ground, he knew that he was doomed. God would exile him, and he would be without his family all the days of his life.

But still he would not repent. *(Taken from Genesis 4:1-16.)*

God Warns Us

Conviction always comes. Sometimes it's through another's warning, sometimes through the very voice of God urging us deep within our souls to humble ourselves and set things right. At every sin there is available the gift of repentance and the ability to prevent even greater damage.

At this moment the enemy makes his bid to control our lives. He whispers in our ears that humbling ourselves will bring bondage to those who have angered us or whom we have wronged. He says that our repentance will give them ammunition to use against us forever—and that is more than we can take.

We judge our ability to survive the rigors of repentance by the weakened, hunted way we feel when guilty—not by the grace of God and His promise of blessing in exchange for our surrender at the cross. We choose our responses from the bottom side up: We see it from the *mortality* of our flesh—not from the *immortality* of our spirits. We worry about the survival of our "dignity" among mortals rather than the health of the only part of us that will live forever. We gain the world but lose our souls.

We foolishly and readily trade our spiritual freedom for one last stand of the corrupted flesh. And like Cain, when sin has brought its harvest, we ask only that we be allowed the comforts of this life a while longer.

If only we would repent of the first offense, those that follow on its heels would not be necessary. If only we believed in our God.

SILENCING THE SPIRIT

Rick stood alone in the middle of the family room of the rambling ranch-style home. Millions of memories were tied in the bundles and boxes piled haphazardly along the walls of the room. Mandy's beloved dollhouse, Jon's report cards that he had proudly kept year after year, his wife Betsy's collection of classical music—box after box bulged with family treasures.

A truck entered the driveway. As Rick turned to leave the room, he nearly tripped over the worn skateboard he himself had played with as a teen. He had passed it on to his son just this year. Regaining his composure, he wound his way out of the room and onto the back patio.

He didn't want anyone to see him here. He had only come to say good-bye to the place before turning the keys over to the new owners. All that remained inside of his wife's and children's belongings would be gone in a few hours, whisked away by the movers who had just pulled up.

He had been fired from Calvary Counseling Center, and now his family was leaving him. God's voice seemed too far away to be heard anymore. His heart felt like it had turned to stone.

When the relationship with his secretary had been discovered, he had broken it off—but he had refused to repent. After all, he rationalized, if Betsy had loved and understood him the way Gayle had, he wouldn't have looked for affection outside the home. It was really *her* fault.

Haven't I given Gayle up? he thought to himself, gritting his teeth. *Wasn't that sacrifice enough?*

But Rick hadn't really given her up. She still played about his mind incessantly, and he looked for her on every street corner. Maybe he'd catch a glimpse of her; maybe it'd be raining and he could give her a lift without anyone seeing them. But she avoided him like the plague.

Before discovery, his conscience had bothered him a great deal, but he had resisted and resisted until its voice could barely be heard. A slow burning anger had replaced it, an anger that he unleashed upon Betsy and the kids at the slightest provocation.

THE POISON OF RESISTANCE

When the refusal to repent lasts long enough, we change. Furthermore, as we build cases against others in an attempt to dodge the guilt, revenge seeps out from our lives, poisoning those we are called to love. We falsely think that denying full responsibility for our sins will halt the sowing and reaping process. We think we will be spared punishment or that it can at least be diluted by demanding that others share in our guilt.

Our minds devise clever ways of balancing the scales to prevent judgment upon ourselves. Offenses of others—real and imagined—bloom noxiously in the fertile soil of revenge. As our anger gains color and texture, reality shifts out of focus. We, in glass houses, think we can throw stones.

But God will not be mocked. What *we* sow, *we* will reap. By tampering with justice we only cause an unnecessary increase in everyone's pain. And because God made the law, our anger may turn toward Him as well. After being filled with the poison of unrepentance, we lose all perspective of who rules the universe. We behave like the drunk who, after injuring someone while driving under the influence, blames the policeman who writes him the ticket. Anger destroys true reason.

THE ONLY WAY BACK

Only the cross can restore sanity and redeem our lives. The forgiveness offered by Jesus' death—and identifying with His brokenness at Calvary—can initiate a spiritual law stronger than natural law. Love—His love for us in the act of substitutionary suffering and the love of family and friends who forgive and offer another chance—covers our sins and rewards us with the miracle of blessing instead of cursing.

In the natural, we deserve the cursing. But the surrender of grievances by the offender and the offended breaks the power of retribution. The pain need not go any further.

THE INSUFFICIENCY OF HUMAN LOVE

In matters of the heart we are particularly prone to the fear that we will not be loved sufficiently during our stay on earth. Most of our pain-producing decisions come from our attempts to secure an abundance of human devotion. But in many cases there never seems to be enough. The truth is often that we have not learned how fully loved and embraced we are by God. As a result, we fix our eyes on those closest to us to fill our cisterns of emotional need. In our quest for affirmation, we often drain the love out of whoever is near simply because we ourselves have run dry. And then, when they don't give affection as freely as they once did, we are annoyed that we should now have to ask for it.

What we fail to realize is that our never-ending selfishness has ruined their capacity to fill us. We haven't replenished their supply by pouring our own love and devotion into them in return. All the natural affection that came to us was taken and not returned. Now we wonder foolishly why there is no spontaneity left.

But beneath the entire dilemma rests one great misunderstanding—that mere mortals can *ever* give us enough love to satisfy or earn unending love from us. Only God can do this. Only His love can withstand insults, slights and neglect.

At the height of mankind's unfaithfulness to Him, God sent His Son to show how much He loves us. He gives us the keys to a kingdom that will never prove fickle nor pass away. His love for us is without question. No command had to be given to Him to love us. In fact, all love was invented by Him and flows from Him.

WE NEED HIS LOVE

But God knew that our greatest dangers would come when we neglected Him, when we fell out of intimacy with Him, when we ceased resting contentedly in His provision of love for us.

Hence, the greatest commandment: We are to love the Lord our God with all our heart, soul, strength and mind—in response to His immeasurable love for us. This would satisfy. This would fill us up on the inside, and out of this would flow love for others. That love would be a good love, reflecting the value He has placed on our lives by cherishing us.

He told us to love Him not because He is greedy or selfish, but because He knew that we would be miserable and empty without the love that only He could give. He knew that if we went through life without loving Him and drinking daily of His love for us, we would torture anyone who dared try to love us enough to replace Him. No other love would satisfy. We are designed to be intimate with Him first, then one another.

He knew that hell would overtake us if we tried to go it alone. Without Him we are lost and undone, only shadows of who we were meant to be when God had us in His eye before we were born.

We Can Begin Again

At the cross—where He graphically demonstrates the distance He will personally go to help us understand the depth and unalterability of His love—we can begin afresh. We can give to Him all our longings for the perfect love and, likewise, all our failure at trying to give any such thing to anyone else.

We can ask for His forgiveness for neglecting Him and for endlessly chasing human love instead of receiving His.

At the cross, as we die to all our cravings—seeing that they have only distracted us from the real thing—our eyes are torn from this earth and its definitions. Our vision rises to heaven, our true home, where love that passes all understanding waits for us.

At the cross we see the seriousness of disobedience. We see the Son of God being brutally murdered by religious zealots who, blinded by their own importance, had lost their way. We see in the resurrection that His love out-powers anything and everyone on this earth and below. We come to understand that His love has never gotten its strength from the amount of love others have given to Him first, but through His intimate and eternal oneness with the Father. Out of that union He can give and give and give.

And so can we. At the cross a divine engagement is announced. We become promised to Him—His bride-to-be. The courtship begins and we learn of true love. Anger and revenge are left behind in sad memories as a new love is born in our hearts. We rise from our knees free of hatred and full of the desire to be reconciled to those we thought disappointed us. We have new eyes and new hearts. Old things have passed away and all things have become "new."

It is in the *why* of the commandments that we grow up. It is because we are all precious in His sight and dearly loved that we do not want to murder or commit adultery—or any of the other sins that hurt those around us. And it is because of His love given at Calvary that we have no trouble loving Him with everything that's in us.

ALWAYS WARNED

As many of us look back on our lives and see the carnage caused by our selfishness in human loving, we may think we had no warning and therefore couldn't have helped ourselves.

But God is just. He always warns us just as He did Cain. Our difficulty arises from not heeding what we didn't want to hear.

NOT TOO LATE

We *can* come to love the warnings and listen for them at every turn. We *can* face life with our eyes wide open, grateful for His grace and delighted to obey Him and have life set right again. One sin no longer *needs* to lead to another. We *can* be freed if we will cease resisting *now*.

CHAPTER NINE

LOVE OF THIS WORLD

Do not store up for yourselves treasures on earth, where moth and rust destroy, and where thieves break in and steal. But store up for yourselves treasures in heaven, where moth and rust do not destroy, and where thieves do not break in and steal. For where your treasure is, there your heart will be also. (Matthew 6:19-21)

Her mind was in a whirl. She and her two daughters grabbed whatever they could carry of the silk and linen, gold and silver treasures before they fled their house in Sodom. Judgment was coming on their city, so said the two strangers who claimed they were sent by God to help them escape.

In spite of all her husband Lot's protests, the strangers propelled the family through the streets, away from the city and toward the mountains.

"Whatever you do, don't look back when the destruction comes," the men stressed.

"Lot! This is foolishness!" his wife protested when they paused to catch their breath. "Our home! Our friends!" she puffed. "How can the Lord be so cruel as to destroy them?" she asked in disbelief and anger. "Everything we worked for will be gone. We'll have to start over!"

Lot didn't answer at first. He was upset too. *Sure,* he thought, *Sodom has practices I don't approve of, but their trade is our bread and butter!*

"Be quiet, woman! Don't make it worse by going on about it," he hissed at his wife.

Turning to the men of God who had rescued them, Lot begged, "Please! A trip to the mountains will kill me! I'm not a young man anymore!"

Knowing that Zoar lay just ahead, he pressed his argument. "How about that village?" he pleaded, motioning toward the little town on the near side of the mountains. "We can be safe there."

"Very well. I'll grant the request and not overthrow the town you speak of," one of the men responded. He looked hard at Lot and continued gravely, "But hurry. I can't do anything until you reach it."

Returning to his wife, Lot gave her the news. "I've persuaded them to let us go to Zoar. People there can help us," he said with relief.

The prospect, however, gave his wife little comfort. Nothing would be equal to what she had left. With renewed strength they walked and ran to the village as sorrow gripped them over their losses. Lot thought of the money, livestock and prestige. His wife longed for her friends, home and finery. Their daughters wept for their fiancés, who had refused to come along.

Just as Lot and his family reached Zoar at sunrise, an ear-splitting explosion came from behind them. Burning sulfur fell from the sky and struck Sodom and Gomorrah. The flames licked the heavens as they devoured the cities and all within them. No one could possibly have escaped!

At the thought of her beautiful city going up in smoke, Lot's wife did what she had been warned not to. With longing in her heart, she turned to look back.

"No!" cried Lot, "Don't look!" But he was too late. His wife suddenly became rigid and still. Her color faded to a ghastly gray; her eyes became fixed in death. *(Taken from Genesis 19:14-26.)*

CHOOSING THE HOME OF OUR TREASURES

When I was a child I learned a delightful song that I came to love. The song was about heaven. It explained to me that this world wasn't really my home. I was only traveling through it for a short season. Furthermore, it said that my treasures were all in heaven—not here on earth—and I began to long for that place.

As a young girl back on my parents' farm, I often climbed the gentle hill behind the house. It led to the hedgerow that followed the slope and defined the field's boundaries. After picking berries from the hedgerow when they were in season, I would walk to the middle of the field and find a soft spot to sit down. There, with tears in my eyes, I'd eagerly search the sky and every cloud, hoping to see Jesus coming to take me Home. How I longed to see Him face-to-face! I don't remember ever worrying about what I would leave behind.

As a teenager I was filled with hopes and dreams for a family and a home of my own. I visited the field less often—until checking the crops with my dad on Sunday afternoons became the only time. But we didn't talk about heaven then—only about the earth and what grew around our feet. I dreamed of whom I might marry, instead of going Home. Later, career and ministry dreams were added. Heaven was something I prayed would wait.

But life has been harder than I had expected—and for this I am actually glad. How easy it can be to love this world when it yields nothing but comfort and plenty! Maybe it is because I am especially weak that God has chosen to keep the world's treasures at a great distance from me. They have mattered little—but even "little" has been too much.

LOSING OUR LONGING FOR HEAVEN

In recent years there have been fewer and fewer songs about heaven in the worship services of many evangelical churches. They seem to be quite unpopular. I went through a period myself when I disdained songs about heaven. It seemed that they were usually sung by people who couldn't come to grips with the difficulties of this life and only wanted to escape their problems. Perhaps I was right in some cases. I imagine also that others preferred to dream of another place where the Holy Spirit would quit challenging them. That seemed easier than applying the cross and surrendering to God in this life.

But I fear that heaven's unpopularity among most Christians today stems from another phenomenon that is gripping this country—and perhaps the entire world. We are looking to our positions *here* as our final places of rulership. We act as if this is all there is!

CENTERED ON OURSELVES

Today, even in the church, we are tempted to root our dynasties in the sod of planet earth. The thought of heaven is disconcerting. Because many of us have drifted away from intimacy with the Lord, where *He* is matters less than where *we* are.

"What will we do there?" we ask. "Will we like it? Will we feel as valuable there as we do here? Will we get what we have always wanted?" We have neglected heaven for so long that we find it hard to eagerly anticipate leaving this place. As we camp out in the shadows of earthly values, we lose our hunger to see Jesus face-to-face.

LOSING OUR FEAR OF HELL

Sermons on hell—like songs about heaven—are vanishing. Hell seems to be an embarrassing conundrum to enlightened, earth-centered, philosophical Christians.

"How could a loving God create a place like hell?" our critics ask. And we struggle uncomfortably trying to answer them.

We have forgotten that His goodness and compassion *require* a place to punish sin. He would no longer be "good" if He abided the horrors we perpetrate upon one another. He would also not be a God we could trust if, after commanding holiness, He settled for blasphemy. Hell is *real* and it is *logical*. As God is all of "good" there is, hell is all of evil there is. There can be no compromise between the two.

People need to hear that *sin* fuels hell, not God. Sin provided the place: far from God. Sin also provided the conditions: eternal loneliness and unimaginable agony apart from the One who loved us most. God, on the other hand, gave His only Son to pay for those sins so that we would not be doomed.

Our Earthly Heritage

We were born separated from God because of the sinful nature we inherited from Adam. That is why this evil world fit so comfortably before we gave our lives to Christ. And that is why we are now in great danger if we find ourselves no longer hungering for heaven and having lost our fear of hell.

When we lose our concern for eternity, we forget that the lost around us have no such luxury. They will face it someday and find that it is real—even if we never told them so. As for us, our choice creates our condition. If we don't want to worship God alone, we get His absence—as well as all that blooms in darkness. When we resist His love, hell begins to overtake us in the shadows.

We don't need to be cast into the literal hell to find ourselves experiencing a measure of it: loneliness apart from God's presence.

Dealing with the World's Logic

Strange things are happening to Western man's reasoning of late. With the rise of relativism in ethics and the decline of moral absolutes, hell seems to be a mite foolish.

"What am I being punished for?" he asks. "I am innocent. I don't think that what I did was wrong." End of case.

I heard a child on the street shout at his mother, "But no one told me I couldn't cheat." Cheating itself brought no twinge of guilt to the boy. The sin was on the part of the person who failed to tell him that cheating wasn't appropriate. If each individual can determine what is right and what is wrong, why not decide that no one deserves hell? If man can determine what God is like and what He might require, why not rule out sin entirely?

When we as believers resist leaving the world and its treasures at the cross, we become like the philosophers of this planet. We, the clay, begin to think that we can shape the Potter. Dangerously like the ancient Greeks and Romans, we will be tempted to create God in our own image so that we can live comfortably with our consciences. We will create a permissive God so that we can convince ourselves that evil will be left unpunished. How absurd!

THE TRUTH ABOUT GOD

God has existed since before time; He cares nothing for our "reasoning." He is not subject to man's fancies. God is absolute goodness, righteousness, holiness, mercy, compassion and love. The vast and absolute God has chosen to bind Himself to us in continual and enduring faithfulness. At the cross He moved heaven and earth to provide a remedy for our darkness. He offered us eternal life in heaven so we would not suffer forever. Such goodness far outstrips the "goodness" modern man wants to attach to God by saying He will tolerate what kills us.

GRAVE DANGER

The shadows of resistance to God's perspective slide over us little by little as we deny Him in the small things.

What do we think we can't live without? What would cause our hearts to nearly stop beating if it were suddenly missing from our lives? From what do we get our identity and our confidence aside from being God's child?

We need to answer these questions. Then, as the fire of the Holy Spirit moves through our hearts, willing to consume whatever has come between us and the joy of an eternity with God, what will we do? Will we surrender them at the cross, or at the last moment look at them with longing and resist again?

CHAPTER TEN

SPIRITUAL ARROGANCE

Woe to those who call evil good
*   and good evil,*
who put darkness for light
*   and light for darkness,*
who put bitter for sweet
*   and sweet for bitter.*

Woe to those who are wise in their
*   own eyes*
*   and clever in their own sight.*
                    (Isaiah 5:20-21)

"Where is he?" Saul worriedly asked no one in particular as he shaded his eyes with his hand and squinted into the afternoon sun, searching for the familiar form of the prophet Samuel. "He was supposed to be here by now!"

To his right, soldiers stirred uneasily, waiting for orders in bedraggled clumps. The murmuring had begun yesterday and was rising to a mutinous pitch today. If the traditional sacrifice wasn't made and God's direction sought soon, every man would desert by nightfall.

They were scared. And well might they be! Camped at Micmash were the Philistines—sporting 3,000 chariots, 6,000 charioteers and soldiers as far as the eye could see. Poised like a tiger about to spring upon the unarmed Israelites, the Philistines' presence filled them with visions of imminent slaughter. If Saul did not take action, not one Hebrew man would be standing at day's end, they were sure.

But King Saul had been given explicit instructions to wait for Samuel before making a move. Only the prophet had the authority to offer the sacrifice and petition God on Israel's behalf. To ignore the command to wait on the holy man was inconceivable.

But so was allowing the enemy to wipe them out in a bloody massacre! They must get battle instructions from God before it was too late!

"That *is* the point, isn't it?" the king said absently to the servant who at that moment happened to bring him a drink of water.

"Your Highness?" the lad responded quizzically. "The point, Your Highness?"

"Doing something before it is too late. Keeping the men from deserting out of fright," answered the king quickly. He turned his eyes to the young man with whom he had inadvertently begun a conversation.

"Yes, I suppose so, Your Highness," the bewildered servant obediently answered and then moved on to serve another officer.

What a faltering start at being king, he mused. Jonathan's troops—not his—had moved gallantly upon the Philistines in the first place; but he, Saul, had taken credit. Now his reputation was on the line as the Philistines amassed to retaliate, and he was not going to be immobilized by Samuel's absence.

"Joash!" Saul barked at one of his men. "Prepare the altar. Bring me the animal for the burnt offering so that we can get instruction from God."

"There," he said to himself, breathing a sigh of relief. "I've done it." To appear tough and in control, Saul offered the sacrifice himself before his troops could act on their mounting fears and desert him.

Saul struck the fire to the sacrifice, and boldly prayed to God for direction.

But just then, as the sun dropped within a foot of the horizon, Samuel appeared. Rising from his knees, Saul strode to meet him. To mask the fear in his heart at having been caught in disobedience by this man of God, he put on his most self-assured face.

Surveying the scene, Samuel was aghast. "What have you done?" he demanded.

Losing confidence fast but struggling to stay in control, he said, "I saw that the men were scattering, and that you did not come at the set time, and that the Philistines were assembling at Micmash," Saul's excuses lamely began. "I thought, 'Now the Philistines will come down against me at Gilgal, and I have not sought the Lord's favor.' So I felt compelled to offer the burnt offering."

Samuel paced in front of the king. Stopping abruptly, he riveted his eyes on the renegade king. He spoke slowly and deliberately so that Saul would understand his message and the gravity of the situation.

"You acted foolishly," Samuel began. "You have not kept the command of the Lord your God. If you had, He would have established your kingdom over Israel for all time."

He continued grimly, "But now your kingdom will not endure. The Lord has sought out a man after His own heart and appointed him leader of His people because you have not obeyed."

Turning on his heels, Samuel took the reins of his donkey and walked away. Saul stood dumbfounded, watching the prophet's disappearing form. Then the king stiffened his back against the fearsome pronouncement. He headed toward his troops. His world would go on—he would see to that! The men were still here—no thanks to the prophet—and in them he would find his strength.

As few as they were, they would persevere—as he would persevere—with or without Samuel's blessing. Surely God would understand. *(Taken from First Samuel 13:1-14.)*

ABUSE OF FREE WILL

Saul's story strikes at the heart of the human dilemma. From Adam and Eve to Saul and on to us today, the battle to call the shots persists. Whether it is from pride or insecurity, our longing for recognition and control eats away at our allegiance to our loving God.

"Surely," we reason, "we must take matters into our own hands. Why else do we have a free will?"

But our arguments fall short of reaching the ears and approval of God. Through all our rationalizations for moving ahead of Him or ignoring His warnings, He calls simply, "Trust Me. Obey Me and all will be well." But we aren't convinced. And in the shadows stands the cross upon which His Son suffered for our actions and attitudes.

The disobedience, pride and determination to rule in God's stead are great in the world at large. But the renegades that wound His heart most deeply are those that call Him "Father."

IMPATIENCE WITH GOD

"More wrinkles." Kathy whined as she ran her fingers over the skin around her eyes while peering in the bathroom mirror. "I'm not *that* old, am I?"

Grabbing her makeup, Kathy applied it carefully to the age spots and wrinkles.

"I'm sick of waiting for God to bring the perfect man into my life," she muttered as she pulled on her stockings and slipped into her shoes. While straightening her dress and putting finishing touches on her hair, a plan began to form in her mind.

"So what if Jack's not a Christian," she said. "The Christian guys in the singles' group at church don't have a clue as to what I want in a man," she added with disdain. "I've been turning Jack down for months, but today my resisting is over," Kathy announced to Mittens, her cat, as she grabbed her car keys and purse and headed for the door.

"A bird in hand is worth two in the bush," she called back to Mittens as she headed out the door for work. By that afternoon Kathy had a date with Jack for Friday night. Within a month, even though she still knew very little about him, his charm had won her heart.

Fighting Conviction

Whenever she felt a warning call in her spirit, she put on one of the CDs that Jack had bought for her and drowned out the Voice with romantic mood music. With each rebuff of the Holy Spirit, Kathy reinforced her deadly choice: She would make up her own rules and disregard God's. But the result was not what she expected.

LOSING GROUND

Kathy's prayer life died and church seemed irrelevant. Her Bible read like ancient history and was soon gathering dust in her closet.

She was like putty in Jack's big, strong hands. One December night he stayed until the sun broke through the clouds the next morning. As she showered for work, Kathy couldn't seem to feel clean, no matter how much soap she used. She beat back the conviction of her sin and argued with God that when they were married, she'd return to Him and bring Jack with her.

By March Jack had moved in with her, but he changed the subject whenever she hinted at marriage. In fact he avoided *any* inquiry Kathy made about his past or plans for the future. His vagueness bothered her, but at the same time intrigued her by its very mystery. She would win him over, she was sure. But the harder Kathy tried to please him, the more distant he became. Then one April morning, Jack was not there. On the pillow next to hers she found only a note that read:

Dear Kathy,

> *I'm sorry. My wife wants me back.*
> *I thought I was over her, but I'm not.*

> *Good-bye,*
> *Jack*

As the note fell from her fingers, huge tears rolled down her cheeks. She turned back to her pillow and buried her face in it as she wept.

Our Misery

The stories of spiritual loss and human sorrow that Christians can tell rival those of the world. The misery we deal ourselves when we refuse to trust God with our futures—when we refuse to wait for Him to fulfill our dreams—is staggering!

Sometimes we're ignorant of the rules; sometimes we are the victim of another's abuse. But more often we simply don't take God's instructions seriously. We hear too little from our elders about purity (perhaps because they are still recuperating from the effects of their own sins) or about choices, grace that enables obedience, the gravity of sin and the rewards of intimacy with God. And even when we do, we too often choose spiritual arrogance.

It's frightening that so many of us have our eyes on the prizes of this world. Immediate gratification is the theme song of this age, and many Christians are singing along.

Spiritual Intimacy Impossible

When we give our hearts to someone who doesn't love God, allegiance to that person becomes a wedge driven between God and us. Betrayal sets up camp in our lives. If sexual intimacy becomes part of the package, we find ourselves losing more than we ever knew we had—while Satan laughs from the pit of hell.

When we marry in rebellion against God, companionship with that person leaves us thirsty, for spirit-to-spirit sharing is impossible with an unbeliever. The loneliness we experienced before meeting this person pales in comparison to the loneliness that we experience after. It feels as though life has ended.

No *man* can heal our wounds and make us whole. No *woman* can nurture enough to make up for self-hatred and anger. Only *God* can deliver us.

And He will, if we will return to the cross.

GOD'S FORGIVENESS AND HEALING

If we are single and have sinned sexually, Jesus is waiting to forgive when we admit our sin and ask Him to wash us clean. If we are married and have committed adultery, He will forgive when we repent. He will give us the grace to bear the discipline that will likely follow and to separate ourselves from the person with whom we had no right to be involved.

If we married for the wrong reasons and are now very unhappy, even this God can redeem. If we will forgive our spouses for not meeting our expectations (just as God has forgiven us), the stage will be set for something amazing to happen. He will call them by the same lovingkindness by which He called us and, if we will render compassion instead of judgment, God can win their hearts.

THE TRUTH

If we feel sorry for ourselves regarding the one whom we are "stuck with" for life, we need a simple revelation: Our mates are likewise "stuck with" us! Considering our ungratefulness and self-righteousness, it is a miracle that they have chosen to put up with us.

You see, self-righteous judging ruins us. When our mates come up short on our self-constructed measuring rod, our arrogance makes us very ugly creatures indeed. Furthermore, sin flowers in the fertile ground of ungratefulness. Jealousy, meanness, slander, adultery and even murder spring from such soil.

The cross reminds us that we are sinners at heart—no better than the worst of those for whom Christ died. It keeps us on our knees where we belong. No matter what our situation, no matter how difficult our choices have made life, God is with us to love us through to victory. The end result is *maturity*—the missing element when we made our choices.

Actually, the one we married is tailor-made to bless us by driving us to the cross! As we lay down our lives in love for our mates, *whether we see them changing or not*, we enter into the sufferings of Christ. When we forgive daily, never letting grudges build; when we answer softly to angry words; when we pray and worship alone; when we serve without thanks and remain faithful and grateful in heart, we are becoming like Him.

Our focus begins to move away from earth and toward heaven, and from our pain into the Father's redemptive plan.

COMPASSION

We finally see our mates with the compassion Christ showed when He died for those who, at the time, had no comprehension or appreciation of what He was doing. But it was for the *joy* set before Him that He endured the cross—the joy of obedience to the Father and of anticipating the defeat of sin in our lives. He died with no one expecting a happy ending, but He knew and trusted the Father. This, with His power, we too can do.

We personally cannot save our mates or change them—but God can. When we stop binding them to failure by our judgments and ungratefulness, God will be able to get their attention. Perhaps God has been convicting them for a long time, but because we have been treating them like an enemy, they have been resisting the Holy Spirit for fear of "losing" the battle and hearing our victory crow! How much better it would be to be our mate's friend, encouraging him or her all the way.

We mustn't be afraid to love them for fear it will appear that we condone their rebellion. God sees; He will convict and change lives. We must stop playing God and begin to truly worship Him as Lord.

WE ARE CHANGED

One thing is certain on this journey of trusting Him all the way to the cross: *we* are changed as we die daily with Christ instead of rebelling in arrogance. We are changed as we begin to see our spouses through Jesus' eyes. We are changed as we come to understand the joy that is set before us and as we endure the cross without grumbling. We are changed as we wait patiently for God's best. We are changed as we cherish *His* plan for our lives which is being made ready to see Him face-to-face.

The breaking of our wills and expectations is not a bad thing. When we have stayed sweet through the crushing, our lives will be an aroma of worship to Him who gave His life for us.

As we withdraw frequently from the press of life to spend time alone with Jesus, we will come to hear His voice and sense His presence and direction. As we grow in our understanding of His love for us, we discover that He satisfies as no other lover *can*. We learn to live for eternity, guarding our hearts from any attachment that could challenge our devotion to the Lord.

AFFECTIONS SET ON JESUS

Whether we are single or married, our affections must first be set on Jesus. He alone will love us perfectly. He alone will be to us a never-ending love song in the night.

And after we humbly follow Him to the cross, wisely and willingly dying to the immediate gratification of our earthly desires and longings, we will have abandoned the shadows and come into His presence.

CHAPTER ELEVEN

JUDGING BY MERE APPEARANCES

But God chose the foolish things of the world to shame the wise; God chose the weak things of the world to shame the strong. He chose the lowly things of this world and the despised things—and the things that are not—to nullify the things that are, so that no one may boast before him. . . . Therefore, as it is written: "Let him who boasts boast in the Lord." (1 Corinthians 1:27-29, 31)

The day had been sultry with barely a breeze to soften the lines in Michal's scowling face. High above the deserted streets in the king's palace at the northern end of Jerusalem, David's wife dampened a towel with cool water from the pitcher on her bedside stand. She patted her neck and face with it to relieve her fatigue as she waited.

All Israel, it seemed, had gone out with her husband to bring the Ark of the Covenant from Obed-Edom's house to Jerusalem, the center of Jewish life these days. She had never seen David so obsessed with anything as he was with establishing worship around the Ark in this city!

"So much fuss over a piece of wood!" she said curtly, biting off each word.

Walking to the open window in her bed chamber, a speck in the distance, approaching from the direction of the Jordan River, caught Michal's eye. Placing both palms down on the sill, she leaned forward, straining to determine if it was David and the people or an enemy expecting to take advantage of the king's absence.

Just as the speck grew into a multitude of marching men, women and children, the sound of their voices reached her ears. Laughter and singing, accompanied by tambourines and trumpets, rang across the plain. Such hilarity Michal had never witnessed before!

As the rejoicing crowd reached the city gates, Michal quickly spotted David. She couldn't miss him. There he was at the front of the parade, dancing and shouting more feverishly than all the rest!

It would have been hard for anyone to have guessed that this dancing fool was royalty! His kingly robe had been shed and his face was flushed from the physical exertion. Young and old milled around him, joining him in praise to God. They also praised God for the Ark which priests carried directly behind the king.

"How can I respect such a man?" she asked herself as she paced the floor of her room, occasionally casting a disgusted glance out the window. "My father would never have lowered himself to dance in the sight of servant girls!" Shaking her head, she declared, "David has no sense of his position. He still acts like a dusty sheep herder!"

THEIR HISTORY

Michal and David had married young, back when he was the brave hero of her father Saul's royal forces. He had won her hand in battle. But it hadn't taken long for her father to become jealous of David and drive him into exile. She had helped David escape by putting a decoy in his bed to mislead her father's guards. How exciting those days had been!

It had soon become evident, however, that King Saul would never allow David to return. To spite David, her father ordered her marriage to another.

As the years wore on, her heart cooled toward the love of her youth and she gave it to her new husband. Then, just as life was becoming somewhat sane, war took the lives of her father and brother. Her life again became one of uncertainty as the tables were turned, and David grew in power.

She had seen it coming, but it broke her heart when the day arrived. She was forcibly taken from the man she had come to love and, in tears, was delivered to the new king of Israel—the husband she no longer loved.

Michal had not grown up with David in the desert during the years when her father had hunted him. She had not watched him turn from a dreamer into a warrior and then into a king through his experiences in the wilderness. His image and pride had taken a beating; it was in the desert that he had learned to trust his God in a way that caused the abandonment in worship that Michal was now witnessing.

David didn't care anymore what people thought. With riches and power waiting for him in Jerusalem, he cared only that God receive praise and glory for the events of this day. If God deserved dance, then he would dance. If God desired praise, David would praise. If God delighted in worship, then this shepherd-king would worship.

Through all the losses and sorrows, victories and joys, David had come to know God.

Michal, on the other hand, had buried her losses and sorrows inside. As a result, she couldn't see into the realm of the spirit and struggled against trusting God as David did. For always, in the shadows, was her resentment toward this God of Israel. Perhaps it was He who was to blame for all her misfortunes.

Her only consolation was the dignity she had as the king's first wife—a new position of prestige she had assumed when she returned to take her rightful place. If there was one thing she had learned from her father, it was the importance of appearing in control.

As she watched in disgust as David carried on like a commoner in the streets below her, she puzzled at how he could care so little about what others thought. She envied his obvious freedom but despised him for having found what seemed to elude her at every turn. *(Taken from Second Samuel 6:12-23.)*

THE RESULT OF KNOWING GOD

As a result of David's deep devotion, God let him "see" the cross prophetically, centuries before it would be erected at Golgotha. He "knew" the pain and suffering the Savior would go through and wrote about it in the Psalms. Because he yielded his heart to God—not to a system or an identity—he was intimate with the God of heaven as no one else at the time was or, perhaps, has been since.

The Holy Spirit expresses Himself and moves in our lives as He wills. At Pentecost the believers who were filled with the Spirit seemed to many to be drunk. Jesus healed on the Sabbath and even put mud on a man's eyes when He healed them. The great King David danced at the thought of worshiping before the Ark of God just as his forefathers had generations before. All these unusual methods brought glory to God.

We must not become spiritual snobs. We must love God *more* than our "positions," traditions, image or style of ministry. We must not fear what people might think. Like David, we must never hide honest emotions nor sacrifice pleasing God in order to please man.

An Unlikely Vessel

The rough-hewn, ex-heroin addict turned preacher pounded the pulpit and then broke into tears.

"God ain't messin' around, you guys! You keep playin' games and frontin' to make others think you're holy, and God will stop protectin' you and let your stinkin' heart take you down!" he pointed a bony finger at the men in the audience. He bore down on them with steel-blue eyes set in a weather-beaten face.

"You hear me, brothers? I ain't here for my health. I'm here 'cuz God's callin' you today to get real!" he shouted.

At that he started stomping and shouting "Hallelujah!" at the top of his lungs. The guys who were new at Teen Challenge sat with their mouths hanging open at this unusual performance from the platform.

I couldn't take any more of his antics and slipped out of my seat at the back of the chapel. I tiptoed from the room and went to my office to prepare for my first class.

MY RESENTMENT

When 9 o'clock rolled around, there were no students in sight. I was getting annoyed. First "Hallelujah Harry"—as staff members had dubbed him—had more than likely scared the new students with his ridiculous antics. And now he was taking up *my* class time! He was invading my territory, and I was offended. Finally, the sound of voices and the rumble of feet in the long hallway between the chapel and the academic wing filtered through to the classrooms. They were coming at last.

"Who knows *what* he did after I left," I muttered to myself as I waited at the front of the classroom. I'd have to apologize and reassure them that Teen Challenge is actually a sensible, sane place despite what they had just witnessed.

But as my students filed into the room and quietly found their seats, I sensed something different in the air. They weren't jostling about and joking with each other as usual; they were almost pensive, lost in reflecting on something serious.

After they were all settled, and I was about to apologize for Hallelujah Harry's unconventional preaching style and bad grammar, a student raised his hand. There were tears in his eyes.

"I just want you and my brothers to know that God convicted me big time this morning," he said. "Harry's sermon opened my eyes to the sin in my heart, and I've finally made things right with the Lord."

Hand after hand went up as several men testified to the powerful effect of Harry's sermon. I was dumbfounded . . . and humbled. I was so grateful that I had not had an opportunity to denigrate Harry. I learned valuable lessons that day.

GOD'S CONCERN

God cares for one thing: Intimacy with us, His children, and the end of sin's control in our lives. He knows the hunger and hurts in our hearts and is ready to apply His Son's death on the cross to set us free and restore us to Him.

God has every right to use unconventional methods and unlikely people to expose Satan's lies and bring conviction. Amazingly, when we too are finally abandoned to Him, we may find ourselves showing emotion or expressing our love in ways that we may have previously considered "undignified." And it will be all right with God.

MERE APPEARANCES

"Appearances" are often determined by tradition and culture, which may fuel feelings of superiority.

But appearances don't reveal the condition of another's heart.

When we fall in love with the cross, when we find our sins forgiven and our lives made clean by His blood, our eyesight is altered. We learn to see aright. We find that the ground is indeed level around the cross. The value of one soul is never greater than another.

Judging by appearances separates believers. Through it we elevate ourselves and ostracize others—often the "Hallelujah Harrys" who, if we let them, could break our hearts for Christ's sake and take us to the foot of the cross where we belong. This is not a defense for careless preaching but a plea for vulnerability and the willingness to be taught by the "least of these," as judged by human standards.

Christ called those who knew that they weren't "hot stuff" and then grew them into mature men whose words shook the world. They died not in competition for glory or prestige but with joy that they had run the race and were going home. Their only glory was in the cross that had saved their lives.

They, like David, simply knew their God and loved Him with abandonment. Of such is the kingdom of heaven.

To Avoid Conviction

Sometimes the judging of others is simply thoughtless snobbery. Sometimes it is because God has spoken to us about something that needs to change in our own lives, and we are resisting. Making fun of someone else is our attempt to get out of the fire ourselves.

When we are tempted to ridicule, we need to check first in the mirror. There is no bigger fool than the one who believes that he is wise enough to know the heart of another when his own heart is courting deception.

CHAPTER TWELVE

COMPROMISE

Do not love the world or anything in the world. If anyone loves the world, the love of the Father is not in him. For everything in the world— the cravings of sinful man, the lust of his eyes and the boasting of what he has and does—comes not from the Father but from the world. The world and its desires pass away, but the man who does the will of God lives forever. (1 John 2:15-17)

For three years each day had dawned clear and cloudless—and this day was no exception. Desperation gripped the land of Israel as the drought prophesied by Elijah to King Ahab dragged on.

King Ahab was a mystery. He was a man who governed and enlarged his kingdom with sound economic and military sense, but one who had no mind of his own when it came to spiritual leadership. He had entered into a politically savvy treaty with the Phoenician king, but had foolishly sealed the agreement with his own marriage to the king's idol-worshiping daughter, Jezebel.

Before Ahab knew it, altars to Baal and Asherah polluted the land of Israel. In brazen disdain, Jezebel slew Jehovah's prophets and appointed 450 of her own to lead pagan rituals that were a stench and a grief to God. Hence, the drought—and the showdown on this, yet another cloudless day. God had sent Elijah to tell Ahab that rain was coming, but first a duel must take place between Elijah and the prophets of Baal. All of Israel gathered on Mt. Carmel for the contest.

As they assembled on the crown of the mountain, Elijah motioned for silence.

His voice rang loud and clear, the words probing and convicting to a man: "How long will you waver between two opinions?" he shouted. "If the LORD is God, follow him; but if Baal is God, follow him!" All was silent as they stood mulling the challenge over in their muddled minds.

SHOWDOWN

So Elijah laid out the game plan. He gave the opportunity to the prophets of Baal to make their sacrifice first, calling on Baal to provide the fire. Then he would do the same, calling on the name of Jehovah. The one who answered would be declared the true God.

After building their altar to Baal and laying pieces of a sacrificial bull upon the wood, the prophets cried out to their god. From morning till noon they asked him to show himself strong by sending fire to consume the offering. But to their shouting and dancing Baal did not respond. The people watched with eyes wide and hearts hammering.

At noon Elijah began to taunt them. "Shout louder!" he said in mock encouragement. "Maybe he is deep in thought, or busy or traveling. Maybe he is sleeping and must be awakened!"

As the prophets raised their voices to a fever pitch, Ahab watched with fear in his heart. He was an Israelite, a descendant of Abraham, Isaac and Jacob, and he had heard the stories of how Jehovah God had led his ancestors miraculously and with great spiritual glory in days gone by.

But Ahab's heart had been too in love with human glory to take Jehovah seriously. He had been too busy amassing territory and power to concern himself with the spiritual leadership his people so desperately needed. It had been easy to let his wife take over that responsibility—and hard to resist her.

But she was not here today, and for a brief moment, Ahab felt free. After the prophets of Baal shamefacedly gave up, Elijah moved to center stage on the mountain. The king almost hoped that he himself could at last see what his ancestors had experienced long ago. Perhaps Jehovah would prove Himself to be all that He had been said to be!

And he was not alone. As the Israelites watched Elijah rebuild the broken-down altar that had once been used to worship God, their hearts hungered to see that there truly was a God in heaven who ruled in righteousness. Many longed to return to their own heritage and to have an end to the disgusting, debasing practices they had endured and condoned ever since Ahab had brought Jezebel to Israel.

After placing the wood and the sacrifice upon the stones, Elijah did the unthinkable. He ordered four large jars of water poured over the offering—three times.

"How will it ever burn now, even if fire does come from heaven?" the people wondered to one another. Ahab watched with bated breath as the man of God knelt humbly before the drenched sacrifice and began to pray.

"O LORD, God of Abraham, Isaac and Israel, let it be known today that you are God in Israel and that I am your servant and have done all these things at your command," the prophet earnestly pleaded. "Answer me, O LORD, so these people will know that you, O LORD, are God, and that you are turning their hearts back again."

Suddenly, a bellowing, blistering column of fire fell from the sky! It burned up not only the sacrifice and the wood, but also the stones and the soil, even licking up the water in the trench that Elijah had dug around the altar.

RECONNECTED TO GOD

With a massive move as by one giant man, the Israelites fell prostrate upon the ground and cried, "The LORD—He is God! The LORD—He is God!"

And Ahab stood speechless in awe before Jehovah for one brief moment . . .

He didn't lift a hand against the people who seized the prophets of Baal and killed them all in the Kishon Valley, relief washing over him for one brief moment . . .

And then, in great torrents, the rains came. The wind drove them across the thirsty land, just as Elijah had prophesied. Drenched to the skin, his breath taken away by the wonder of it all, Ahab felt strangely reconnected to the faith of his forefathers for one brief moment . . .

And perhaps the next day, as he told Jezebel all that had happened, he hoped that she would believe with him. But she didn't. Her fury knew no bounds as she determined to find and kill Elijah. Perhaps Ahab resisted her plans for one brief moment . . .

Only once more in his lifetime did he humble himself before God, and then perhaps only to save his own life. In all other cases it has been said of him that "There was never a man like Ahab, who sold himself to do evil in the eyes of the LORD, urged on by Jezebel his wife." *(Taken from First Kings 18:16-46; 19:1-2; 21:25, 27-29.)*

AHAB KNEW BETTER

Volumes could be written about Jezebel—her controlling spirit, her ruthless pursuit of her own agenda and the bitterness in her own heart. But Jezebel was at least committed to what she believed. She was obnoxious and evil to the core, but she never hesitated in her devotion to her gods. She never wavered.

There is even less that is righteous about Ahab. The king knew better. He knew about the God of his people; he had heard the prophets' warnings about the wrath of God coming upon the evil he was allowing through his wife. He knew that as king of Israel he was commissioned to lead spiritually by example—committed in reverence to the laws of God.

REBELLION OF COMPROMISE

But King Ahab looked the Almighty in the eye and continued to sin. He had listened to and believed the same song and dance that Eve had back in the Garden of Eden. *Surely God would not kill me for my rebellion,* he thought. *God did not mean what He said.* He remade God in his own image and then cast Him aside, choosing to worship himself instead, putting his own conquests and glory on a pedestal above the Holy One of Israel.

It repeatedly took "an act of God" to bring him to his knees. But even then, he kneeled on only one knee. The other remained ready to spring into action on Ahab's own behalf. As the silhouette of the cross fell back in time upon him, he argued that it was but a brief illusion, a temporary delay in the pursuit of his own dreams.

Battle for Self-worth

Whap. As the wheels of the huge transport passed his BMW, it heaved sheets of slush onto his windshield as he pressed on down the highway to his next appointment. Visibility cut to zero, Corey grabbed for the windshield wiper knob. As the wipers cleaned the half-melted ice and snow from before his eyes, he breathed more easily and was once again in control.

He glanced at the clock on the dash. Twenty-five minutes to reach Harrisburg. He was banking on closing the deal on the new computer system he was selling to Harmac, Inc.

"Another custom-made deal by the one and only Corey Vandercliff. Ta-da!" He boasted aloud to himself as another splat hit his windshield, and the wipers strained once more to remove the mess so that he could see.

Looking out at the gray rolling landscape, he began to reflect. "How many times have I driven this route?" he mused. "And how many times have I driven routes that look just like it?" Sadness stole over him as visions of endless lonely miles played across his mind.

Then brightening, he spoke to the empty seat next to him. "Hey, Dad, I've done it! Aren't you proud of me?" Corey straightened up and donned his most dignified air. "I told you I'd be rich and famous someday, and I am." Then turning away from his imaginary passenger he ruefully mused, "Well, a little rich and famous anyway."

This one-sided conversation was going nowhere. Boasting to his dad was never very satisfying. His father cared little for financial conquests; he had only encouraged Corey to love the God he loved and to walk in the ways Corey had been taught as a child. This would have pleased his dad beyond measure.

Now, Corey *believed* in that God—but to let Him into the deepest recesses of his heart and give up the outcome of his life? No. No way could he do *that*. The very thought made him grip the steering wheel until his knuckles went white. He would *not* give in. Always before him like a carrot on a stick were tantalizing new things to experience and fascinating places to go. He couldn't risk missing them by allowing God to dictate his adventures.

ON HIS TERMS

But deep inside he longed for God's approval, just as he had longed for his dad's. Why couldn't they both celebrate *him* and his accomplishments? Why couldn't they be awed by all he'd done? Why wouldn't they give him the admiration he craved? What more must he do to get them to approve of him—on his terms?

And Janet was no better. Why couldn't she be thankful for the lifestyle he'd given her? Instead, she was always nagging him to stay home more with her and the kids and be the spiritual leader of the family.

"When they graduate from college without debts hanging over their heads, they'll be glad," he said aloud, trying to persuade himself that his long absences had a redemptive side. "How old are they now?" His brows were knit and his forehead furrowed as he tried to remember. "Mike must be fifteen and Jill, twelve." Then laughing a bit uncomfortably, he added, "I think that's about right."

To arrest the melancholy mood that threatened to grip him as he maneuvered his car along the slick and dismal highway, he snapped on the radio. The DJ's cheery voice broke through his introspection.

"Good morning, America. And now another oldie but goodie coming your way. For all you businessmen, 'The Cat's in the Cradle' . . ."

In disgust Corey snapped the radio off before the song could begin.

Denial of Self

> Then Jesus said to his disciples, "If anyone would come after me, he must deny himself and take up his cross and follow me. For whoever wants to save his life will lose it, but whoever loses his life for me will find it. What good will it be for a man if he gains the whole world, yet forfeits his soul?" (Matthew 16:24-26)

This Jesus said to His disciples after rebuking Peter for having his mind set on the things of earth rather than the things of God. And before long, He demonstrated it on the cross. There He chose devotion to His heavenly Father over a kingdom that He could have built with His hands.

Our cross is a matter of whom we will serve. It cuts a definitive vertical slash between us and every other thing we might want to put first in our lives.

And God as well can stand on only one side in the battle for our lives. He will unflaggingly endorse righteousness and confront sin. It is an all-or-nothing deal in His eyes.

No Compromise

The cross requires a brutal choice and defies any attempt we might make to build and maintain the kingdom of self while trying at the same time to bear His colors. Yet the cross resounds with mercy—mercy on those who may yet heed His voice and surrender, coming out of the shadows and into His presence.

Ahab and Corey, living millennia apart in time, *could* have begged for the hand of God to slay their egos and take their fortunes in return for clean hearts and singular devotion. Their minds *could* have been persuaded, their motives recrafted to agree with God.

But instead either or both may have counted on their godly heritages to rescue them at the last minute. Or perhaps they had reached the conclusion that they were beyond repair, that they had been gone from "home" too long, that no one would recognize or welcome them even if they did return.

TRAGIC LOSS

This misperception of mercy is sad. But even more so is a leader—of a nation or of a family—who wavers between two opinions and provides his followers and offspring no spiritual protection. Israel fell under Jezebel's control, and worshiped abominable gods. And Corey's children, filled with wounds of their father's perceived rejection, sought father figures in the world that promised them power and prominence in return for absolute control over their lives.

When the world is loved, the Father is hated. There is no middle ground. And when the Father is hated, the enemy has won in our lives—no matter what our heritage.

CHAPTER THIRTEEN

LOVE OF MONEY

For the love of money is a root of all kinds of evil. Some people, eager for money, have wandered from the faith and pierced themselves with many griefs. (1 Timothy 6:10)

They came from everywhere—Galilee, the Decapolis, Jerusalem, Judea and the region across the Jordan. Men, women and children abandoned their tasks and their play to follow this amazing Man who could heal the sick and raise the dead.

Such authority He had! As He taught, their encounter was with truth, and that truth was setting their spirits free. No teaching of the Pharisees had ever satisfied their inner hunger and thirst as this Man's did.

When Jesus spoke, each word seemed to come from the tested humility of who He was. The people ate and drank of His life as they listened. They sensed the love within His authority, and they stretched to grab hold of that love.

While the Pharisees taught about spiritual matters with a self-enhancing air of privileged knowledge, this Man Jesus lifted the veil and showed them the Father while seeking no praise for Himself. He behaved as a servant, giving of Himself as freely as He gave of truth.

As He spoke, the law made sense, for they saw its purpose at last—*to show their inability to keep it*. They needed a Savior. The burden was lifted while at the same time a higher call was issued: to live by *His* life, not their own, to lose themselves in obedience to God and love for one another, and to grow in wisdom while pursuing innocence.

The crowd's attention was riveted to this unassuming bearded Man clad in simple robe and sandals. Bearing the heat of the day along with them, with His probing eyes and authoritative voice, Jesus compassionately sought their hearts.

"No one can serve two masters," He said loud and clear. "Either he will hate the one and love the other, or he will be devoted to the one and despise the other." He paused and then calmly, gravely struck at the root of Israel's pride: "You cannot serve both God and Money."

The crowd was puzzled. Most of them were poor. How could they be serving money? What control could money have over them—beyond their need of it—that would require them to deny it to serve God?

What did money represent? What has it always represented to the human race? *(Taken from Matthew 6:24; 7:28-29.)*

CURRENCY OF POWER

Money is earth's currency of power and self-sufficiency. It represents strength because it gives the possessor the ability to purchase whatever he desires, remaining independent of others. If a man has enough money, he can intimidate the world. He needs no one and is envied for his sheer autonomy. But this makes his flesh so fat that he cannot enter the narrow gate.

Loving the power that money can buy has cast mankind as an antagonist of God since the beginning, for autonomy flies in the face of the Creator. Even in the Garden of Eden, while there was no money to entice Eve, there was a means to self-sufficiency: the knowledge of good and evil. This knowledge represented ultimate power to Eve at the moment of temptation. It touched her desire to be like God.

In every age something represents man's quest for ultimate dominance—that which feeds his pride and exerts authority over others.

But Jesus would have none of this.

GOD'S VALUE SYSTEM

"Blessed are the poor" . . . who leave pride and self-promotion behind. "Blessed are those who mourn" . . . who grieve over others' losses and the sad state of the world. "Blessed are the meek" . . . who have surrendered personal power to the control of the Spirit. "Blessed are those who hunger and thirst for righteousness" . . . who understand and long for the currency of heaven. "Blessed are the merciful" . . . who seek to bend down in compassion at the moment of another's greatest weakness. "Blessed are the pure in heart" . . . who are washed clean of selfish ambition. "Blessed are the peacemakers" . . . who yield their own "rights" to ease another into an understanding of the higher call of love. "Blessed are those who are persecuted for righteousness" . . . who see themselves as part of a greater cloud of witnesses and are willing to die for the truth (see Matthew 5:3-10).

Such a gospel offends the religious and non-religious alike who seek power and prestige in this world. It will ultimately shine the spotlight on those bent on self-enhancement, exposing their arrogance.

GRASPING FOR SPIRITUAL POWER

Crowds stood spellbound as he worked his clever deceptions before them day after day. Simon the Sorcerer understood power and never ceased reveling in it.

But one day, while listening to Philip preach, the "Pied Piper of Samaria" became a believer in Jesus and was baptized. Instead of being the followed, he became a follower, trailing Philip wherever he went. Ah, the miracles performed at the hand of this straightforward, uncompromising evangelist! And, as the practiced magician could easily tell, there were no tricks behind the scenes. The former spellbinder became spellbound by the power of God.

When Peter and John arrived in Samaria to minister the gift of the Holy Spirit to all who had been saved at Philip's preaching, Simon was on the scene. As Peter and John laid their hands on the new believers and the Holy Spirit fell upon them, Simon's heart leapt with excitement. This power he wanted, and he offered money to buy it.

"Give me also this ability so that everyone on whom I lay my hands may receive the Holy Spirit," Simon pleaded.

Peter fired back, "May your money perish with you because you thought you could buy the gift of God with it!" Then, Peter's eyes piercing Simon's, he continued. "You have no part or share in this ministry because your heart is not right before God.

"Simon," Peter spoke sternly, "repent of this wickedness and pray to the Lord. He will forgive you for having such a thought in your heart."

Then, in an instant of spiritual discernment, Peter saw the cause of Simon's blindness. "For you are full of bitterness and captive to sin," he concluded sadly. *(Taken from Acts 8:19-23.)*

A TRAP

The world tells us that power and money are easy bedfellows, one refreshing the other. Jesus tells us that loving money not only alienates us from God's presence but make us enemies of His power.

We can love money just as deeply with *or* without it. Intimacy with God is damaged by the degree to which we consider it important. If we have it, we may try to use it to circumvent dependence upon God. If we lack it, we may use that as an excuse to remain in bondage to fear of suffering, of the future and of being in want. Either way, we miss the challenge of the cross—that we trust only Him day by day.

When we measure our availability or worth by the amount of money we have, we lose sight of what happened on the cross. We miss the fact that the wealth of the universe, embodied in the only begotten Son of God, has been spent for us. With our eyes fixed upon dollar bills and silver coins and our vision controlled by how much or little we have, we fail to witness the most costly trans-action of all time.

Icy Gray Shadows

Fear and bitterness slip in like icy gray shadows, dimming and distorting our perception of God's love. If we lack, we worry and doubt Him. We re-fuse to step out in obedience to His commands because of the little we have in our own hands. We dare think that the scope of His power in our lives is bridled by our lack—while, indeed, it is bridled only by our misplaced confidence in what will not last.

If we have abundance, we may fear its disap-pearance if we obey God. What if He does not value our wealth as dearly as we do? We become possessive and suspicious; we hoard our monies and trust them to keep us in peace tomorrow. But because fortune can be fickle, even *with* it we fear being without.

If we are ever to become intimate with Him, our minds must be governed by obedience, so that when God says "move," we will—with or without the appearance of wealth. And as we obey, and demonstrate our belief in His provision, we will begin to take up our cross and follow Him.

HIS EXAMPLE

Jesus lived daily in the tension of owning the cattle on a thousand hills but having no place to lay His head. He never expected anyone to understand. He simply saw beyond this world's financial restriction to the Father who would meet His needs one day at a time as He was obedient. He calls us to do the same.

CHALLENGED BY HIS PRESENCE

Rob hadn't really wanted to attend the missions conference, but his wife Elena had begged him to go with her. And now his heart was burning uncomfortably within him as Alexi Peternov, a young Russian pastor, pleaded for help in the forgotten wastelands of northern Russia. Elena looked at him with tears in her eyes, evidently feeling the same conviction as he.

INFLUENCED BY ANOTHER'S OPINION

Quickly, Rob turned his head away and began counting the windows in the wall, determined to ignore her as well as the pastor. As Rob struggled to understand the stirring in his spirit, he was startled to hear in his imagination his father's crusty voice from out of the past.

"Only *idiots* go to mission fields. Preaching to poverty-stricken pagans is for men who can't make it in the States," sneered the words that had kept Rob out of Bible school and off the mission field.

His father's voice continued, "Let God send someone else." Noticing his crestfallen son, he condescendingly added, "When you're established in a successful law practice, you can use a little of your money to finance another guy."

But he never seemed able to spare money for missions, no matter how successful his practice. There was always something more important.

AFRAID TO TRUST

Now God was calling *him* to go. He squirmed in his seat. *I'd be a fool to give up my career to go to the other side of the world,* Rob reasoned. The thought of following God into the unknown was frightening. He broke out into a cold sweat as scenes of deprivation flooded his mind. *I can't trust Him that much!* he thought.

The burning in his heart eased up and faded away. Rob cleared his throat in relief.

He was back in control.

GOD DEALS WITH US

With or without a given amount, we can be slaves to money if we give it the power to make us self-protective and fearful, or bitter toward God or others. With or without it we can be disobedient children. The amount of money we have means nothing.

But surely, if it means too much to us, He will deal with us. For our very lives' sake, He will move heaven and earth to shake the love of it from our hearts. Then we will be able to turn our eyes—and our faith—toward Him and begin obeying with sweet abandonment.

Then, as we die to the power and control that had previously seemed so essential, the cries of those in need will capture our hearts. And if—as we minister to them in Jesus' name—God's power is displayed, we will take no credit for it. We had nothing with which to buy it, so its ownership remains clear.

And if we have plenty of earth's riches and we freely give unto others as God instructs, we will receive it back multiplied. But we won't notice the return—for we will be lost in the delight of the giving!

As we step out of the shadows of resistance, with our autonomy and self-sufficiency finally dead and gone, we will be right where we can be most dearly used and blessed—completely dependent upon the One who paid the ultimate price to redeem our sorry lives. And His presence will be close at hand.

CHAPTER FOURTEEN

FORGIVENESS REFUSED

If we confess our sins, he is faithful and just and will forgive us our sins and purify us from all unrighteousness. (1 John 1:9)

Early in the morning, all the chief priests and the elders of the people came to the decision to put Jesus to death. They bound him, led him away and handed him over to Pilate, the governor.

When Judas, who had betrayed him, saw that Jesus was condemned, he was seized with remorse and returned the thirty silver coins to the chief priests and the elders. "I have sinned," he said, "for I have betrayed innocent blood."

"What is that to us?" they replied. "That's your responsibility."

So Judas threw the money into the temple and left. . . .
(Matthew 27:1-5)

Judas ran blindly, pursued by the ghastly nightmare he had brought upon himself. Suffocating guilt engulfed him as he fled the city and made his way to a wilderness grove where he could suffer in privacy. His shoulders convulsed with sobs as he fell to his knees to catch his breath, his heart a burning fire about to ignite his whole body.

He hated himself and burned with humiliation.

Judas thought back over the months before, searching desperately for justification to betray

Jesus. Only a helpless feeling washed over him. Nothing had made sense. . . .

"Jesus was doing *nothing* to destroy our enemies," he argued with himself. "What had He meant by, 'a kingdom not of this world?' " he asked in exasperation. "What can a man make of such a fantasy?"

He wiped the sweat from his forehead and continued his dialogue with himself as the sun rose in the morning sky. "Sure, a denarius in a fish's mouth to pay the taxes made an interesting story, but what would they have done the next time if Jesus chose *not* to produce the money?

"The man was totally unpredictable. Nothing seemed to go as it should," he muttered miserably.

Deep inside the singular conversation went on. "But to purposely undo Jesus, to vent my frustration by ripping destiny from His hands . . . for a handful of coins?" The tears fell afresh as he rubbed his hands on his robe as though to clean them from the stain of the blood money they had recently held. In the light of day everything appeared so different.

"What was I thinking? How could I betray the only Man who ever saw anything in me—who trusted me and loved me?" his sobbing dropped to a weak and weary whimper as he remembered the look in Jesus' eyes when he, Judas, had appeared leading the soldiers and officials to Jesus in the garden.

"He loved me still," he whispered. "How I grieved Him!"

Then biting his lower lip so hard that it drew blood, Judas breathed these words: "I don't deserve to live. I am an irredeemable fool!" Saying it seemed to make it so.

The faces of the other disciples took shape in his imagination, haunting him. Perhaps they were under arrest themselves by now.

Self Condemned

"I have ruined everything!" he cried. "There is no hope for me. No one can save me from this horror and disgrace."

A chilling thought began to rise out of the depths of his soul, driven by remorse and self-pity.

"I must die." He ran through the trees, tripping over roots. Only the brambles that clutched at his robe slowed him as he fought his way to the ravine that ran along the edge of the grove.

As he reached the precipice, his heart beat wildly. He tore off the leather belt from about his waist and tied one end around a sturdy tree branch that overhung the ravine. With sweaty fingers he awkwardly knotted the other end around his neck.

With one leap, all went black. As his lungs collapsed, his heart fell silent. It was over. *(Taken from Matthew 26:14-16, 46-49; 27:1-5.)*

Questions Remain

Why didn't Judas seek Jesus' forgiveness before Jesus died? What caused him to isolate himself so totally from the teachings of Jesus that he had heard for three years? Did he think of himself as unique—believing in the Messiah but still having to save himself somehow? Had he missed the message so completely?

It is amazing how often we, who have walked with Jesus for years, and to whom others look for spiritual leadership, have also split the gospel in two: confession, repentance and forgiveness for the masses; but remorse, bitterness and self-destruction for *us*. Could it be a matter of pride?

While there should be great concern in the Church over "cheap grace"—teaching that God issues a blanket forgiveness with or without confession and repentance—there is also the problem of expecting ourselves never to sin and then coming unglued when we do.

"For all have sinned and fall short of the glory of God" (Romans 3:23). Not one of us will live out our days perfectly with our hearts always right. Over and over we will bruise the heart of God; we desperately need to be undressed in confession and bathed in forgiveness. Refusing to humble ourselves under the hand of God and before others can be the death of us—for all the wrong reasons.

CANNOT FREE OURSELVES

Self-flagellation smacks of the heresy that the cross is simply not enough to free us. Yes, Jesus' death and resurrection brought salvation for others, but it was certainly not powerful enough to redeem *us*. We must punish ourselves forever. Or if the sin is great enough in our eyes, we must surely die for it. Forgiveness and grace are too common for us—and we are too *uncommon* for the cross.

Instead of admitting our wickedness, we insist that we were too good for such a sin; therefore our suffering must be unusual. Some of us may get stuck in the denial stage; others of us bound ahead in one mighty leap to the final stage of mounting the cross as our own savior, convinced that our death will right the records. We are so above grace that we think that we can actually become a martyr—for *sinning*.

His Life within Us

Sometimes in our quest to be holy we forget that it is only *His* life within us—through no righteousness of our own—that makes it possible to reflect God's character. And that reflection is as close as we can ever come to being God. In fact, as our estimation of ourselves drops and that of Jesus increases, His image is released in us proportionately. John the Baptist put his finger on a spiritual reality when he said, "He must become greater; I must become less" (John 3:30).

Similarly, the apostle Paul's effectiveness at presenting the gospel, and his own intimacy with God, hinged upon his understanding that it was "Christ in you, the hope of glory" (Colossians 1:27).

At His feet we will recognize daily our need of grace to enable us to release our pride and submit one more time. We will never become too important, too spiritual or too close to God to be above falling to our knees in confession and repentance. We will never refuse grace, and the sweet humbling that comes before it floods our lives, restoring hope.

We sin—often as heinously after having walked with God for a long time as we did when newly converted. And Jesus' forgiveness is as fresh and powerful today when we repent as it was then.

NEVER TOO LATE

Forgiveness and restoration is God's reply to all our sins, no matter how grievous in our sight. Our ranking of sin reveals our lack of respect for the price Jesus paid on Calvary and the sure effect of His blood to redeem us from *every* sin.

Are we greater than God that we should judge His forgiveness insufficient for what we have done? Is *our* death more redemptive than Christ's on Calvary that we should destroy ourselves instead of accepting His sacrifice?

Not receiving His forgiveness for even the worst sin we confess is a curse to the cross. Self-flagellation is actually a perverse form of self-worship, fixing our eyes on ourselves for deliverance from guilt and remorse as though we were comparable to Christ.

Furthermore, if we have confessed and repented and if we know that we are forgiven by God, by no means have we the right to withhold forgiveness from ourselves. Who are we to insist upon leveling punishment upon ourselves when God Himself holds no memory of the sin He has already forgiven?

A MODERN TRAGEDY

As the young man slowly pulled the needle out of his arm, euphoria rolled over him, washing the stress from his muscles. His mind floated on a cloud of fluffy vapor out of his body and into the sky. A tugboat horn sounded eerily in the distance.

But this was not what he had wanted. This time was supposed to be different. This time he had meant to die!

Struggling to pull his mind back to the task at hand, he weakly urged himself, "Do it again. One more hit will do the trick." But he couldn't get his hands to act right. The syringe fell out of his grip and onto the dirty floor of the deserted waterfront shack.

"I can't even do this right," he mumbled miserably.

Tom somehow got to his feet and managed to stumble to the door and out onto the wharf. A short distance away was the bridge that spanned the channel at the mouth of the bay. The water slapped rhythmically against the buoys anchored below as he made his way to the center of the bridge.

As he dropped over the rail into the gray waves below, his last thought was of his mother. His heart broke.

THE WEIGHT OF GUILT

Tommy had been a handful for his mom to raise. After her divorce he had felt uncomfortable in the church youth group and out of place even at home. He had asked Jesus to be his Savior many years ago, but after losing his dad, the pull of the crowd had become too much for him to resist.

Deep inside he had feared that his dad's leaving had somehow been his fault. Tommy thought that perhaps if he had been a better son, maybe his dad would still be here.

He hadn't meant to get into drugs. It had just "happened." It seemed like everybody at school did them, and he couldn't say no. He wanted to fit in. But when he found himself unable to stop and began stealing from his college fund to support his habit, he knew he was in over his head.

But his pride wouldn't let him go to anyone for help. He was too ashamed—especially to face his mom after all she had been through.

Then his girlfriend Megan said she had had enough. She broke up with him last Sunday, cutting the final thread of purpose for his life. Bitterness and disappointment had overwhelmed him. He had been handling his life for so long on his own that he never thought to call out to God.

FORGIVENESS BRINGS HEALING

Many of our lives have become as disjointed as those in the world. Divorce and abuse are nearly as prevalent in Christian homes as in those where

Christ as Savior is unknown. It is critical that we learn from our failures, rebuilding and seeking to walk the way of the cross. At the same time, we must teach and live forgiveness.

As we are open before God about our sins—repenting and receiving forgiveness—we must be open before our children. The betrayals and rejections they have suffered, if they remain undiscussed and unhealed, give rise to self-hatred and false guilt.

They mistakenly think that our sins are their fault. Add that weight to the hurts that they already have, and without forgiveness they will subconsciously plot a plan of revenge upon themselves.

The anger we often see in our children is rooted in their inner protest against the feeling that they are bearing all the blame. They somehow believe in their hearts that there is mercy *somewhere*, but their minds are convinced that self-destruction is the only route to freedom.

KEEN SENSE OF JUSTICE

Young people have a very keen sense of justice. Whether they know God or not, they are convinced that *someone* must pay for sin. Since they are torn by such ugly anger resulting from unresolved wounds, they think that they are the ones who should pay.

But all the while their spirits plead for the Savior. If they are not taken to Jesus—and if they see that the adults in their lives are not about to repent—they will turn upon themselves. In their minds justice must be done. Someone must die.

Teens know deep down that the guilt is not being shared as it ought, but they see no chance of that happening. Amid the hopelessness that overwhelms them, they commit suicide. They die for the sins of the world.

Even beyond the loss of their lives, the greatest tragedy is that their deaths accomplish nothing except to increase the weight of guilt on those that remain.

No One Beyond His Reach

If only forgiveness were taught more thoroughly. Not a mere social amenity that lacks deep repentance on the part of the sinner, but forgiveness that identifies with the sinner and carries him to the arms of our loving Lord.

Forgiveness is accompanied by compassion and restoration. It comes alongside to help change the future. A new day dawns.

For there is *no* sin whose stain His blood cannot remove; there is *no one* beyond the reach of His love. It is His will that we *all* come out of the shadows of resistance and into His presence . . . by way of the cross.

CHAPTER FIFTEEN

COWARDICE

If you are insulted because of the name of Christ, you are blessed, for the Spirit of glory and of God rests on you. If you suffer, it should not be as a murderer or thief or any other kind of criminal, or even as a meddler. However, if you suffer as a Christian, do not be ashamed, but praise God that you bear that name. For it is time for judgment to begin with the family of God; and if it begins with us, what will the outcome be for those who do not obey the gospel of God? (1 Peter 4:14-17)

In hushed voices, the arrangements were made. Pilate granted Joseph of Arimathea custody of the body of Jesus as soon as it was taken down from the cross. Pilate was uneasy about the events of the day. He was more than happy to have someone assuage his conscience by giving a dignified burial to the man he still felt was innocent.

Joseph met Nicodemus, as planned, after everyone else had gone home to prepare for Passover. In the waning light of day, the two men tenderly gathered up the broken and bloodied body of Jesus and carried it a short distance from the site of the crucifixion to prepare it for burial. In accordance with Jewish custom, they wrapped the body, along with the costly spices that Nicodemus had brought, in strips of white linen.

Joseph and Nicodemus were prominent Pharisees and members of the ruling Jewish council, the Sanhedrin. They had found one another by recognizing the look in the other's eyes. Both believed that Jesus was the Son of God; but both were also full of fear.

No scorn was like that of a Pharisee against one of his own who became a "heretic." It could mean not only judgment and ostracism, but their deaths, as well. They knew that the convictions that were forming within their hearts were dangerous beyond imagination, so they kept silent.

Perhaps if they could do some physical service for Jesus, even after His death, they could make up for their hedging during His life.

Their hearts ached as they silently prepared the battered body. Neither could shake his memories. Nicodemus' mind went back to many months earlier when he and Jesus met for the first time—under the cloak of darkness.

How startled he had been at Jesus' opening words, "I tell you the truth, no one can see the kingdom of God unless he is born again." They had mystified Nicodemus.

"How can a man be born when he is old?" he had blurted out. "Surely, he cannot enter a second time into his mother's womb to be born!"

And then, patiently and gently, Jesus had explained spiritual rebirth, the love of God for him and how he could experience forgiveness of his sins and have eternal life with God.

He could still hear Jesus' voice as He unveiled truth that night. "For God so loved the world that he gave His one and only Son, that whoever believes in Him shall not perish but have eternal life," the Master had said as He looked Nicodemus squarely in the eyes.

By the time Nicodemus left Jesus that night, truth had pierced his heart. But he still had many questions. In the days following, he had gradually surrendered his life to this Man from Galilee. He *knew* deep in his heart He was the Son of God. After studying afresh the words of the prophets, he became convinced that He was indeed the long-awaited Messiah.

PIERCED BUT HESITANT

But Nicodemus had kept his convictions to himself. Only once had he dared speak up for Jesus to the council. And then it was only a feeble plea for them to give Jesus a proper hearing before condemning Him.

Joseph had also followed at a distance, letting only trusted friends know of his faith in this Jesus. He had seen Jesus attacked and done nothing to defend Him or to absorb the pain with Him. That conflict now tore at his heart. Now that Jesus was dead, perhaps he could sort things out.

"The tomb is just over there," Joseph said, breaking the silence as the two men carefully secured the last linen strip around Jesus' head. "Help me carry Him there, and we'll be done," his voice broke as his eyes filled with tears. His love for Jesus overwhelmed him for a moment.

Nicodemus nodded, unable to speak. He too was fighting to control his emotions.

Without another word, they carried the body into the burial cave and reverently laid Him on a large, flat stone slab. They could barely see in the dark and musty cave, but neither lit a torch for fear of discovery.

They finished and slipped away to their homes just as Roman soldiers were sent to seal and guard the tomb.

STAKES WERE HIGH

The Jewish religious world had been turned upside down. Those who had previously been in control—with life neatly packaged and securely labeled—were shaken by this man called Jesus. His teachings baffled them. How could the poor be rich, the weak be strong, foolishness be wisdom and losers be winners? How could the kingdom of God be made up of such as these? It was disconcerting, at the very least, for the rich, strong, wise and the religious "winners" in the Jewish culture—especially the scribes and the Pharisees.

They had come to believe their own rhetoric—that they were the keepers of the Law, defenders of the faith, the judges of others, holy men, instructors who were above instruction. The system was safe and risk-free for them—and they would kill to preserve it. Joseph and Nicodemus both knew this. The thief on the cross had nothing to lose in believing; for them the stakes were high.

They were in the vanguard of prominent men who would, in time, respond to the call of the cross. They would follow Jesus publicly—regardless of the price.

But at the time of Jesus' death, they were alone and not ready to count the cost. *(Taken from John 3:1-21; 19:38-42.)*

THE FINAL CHALLENGE

What would *we* do if we too were alone and in grave danger for believing in Jesus Christ? What will we do if—or *when*—that day comes in our lifetime, perhaps in our country?

After the resurrection, believers were stalked and murdered in the name of God. When *His* power was made sure, all hell broke out against the redeemed. When the revival for which we are crying comes to the Church in America, perhaps *we* will be stalked and murdered as well—if not in deed, then in reputation.

SCORNED BY THE WORLD

Could it be that we who are respected now for being upright may yet become the poor, weak, foolish losers that the world will scorn and ostracize?

Reverence toward the Church is fast dropping, whether we personally have earned the scorn or not. The world has seen our many double standards and our lack of repentance. We desperately need revival! We must humble ourselves so that the Holy Spirit can bring resurrection life to His body once again.

COURAGE OR COWARDICE

But when He does, when revival and the shaking comes (see Hebrews 12:26-28), the gates of hell may open against us. Will we stand and be counted in that day? Could we not begin practicing for it now?

When persecution comes, will we proclaim the redeeming power of the cross or look for the bloodied bodies of martyrs to wrap in the twilight?

COMPASSION LOST

"That horrid woman spent the night next door at Betty's again," Susan said with disgust over breakfast the next morning. Bill grunted in reply, his face buried behind the morning paper.

"Bill!" Susan fairly shouted at him. "Betty's a lesbian, I just know it." A shudder ran through her as she made her pronouncement.

Irritated, Bill dropped his paper to his lap with a suddenness that startled his wife. "So? What do you expect me to do about it?" he glared at her over his spectacles. "Shall we move every time we don't like how our neighbors live?" Erecting the paper wall again, he continued, "Who are we to interfere in what someone else chooses to do?" And then he added, mumbling, "It's a free country."

"If only Betty'd go to church and get saved," Susan finished lamely. "She needs help, but I haven't a clue as to what I should do about it."

Susan rose from the table, carrying her dishes over to the sink. She rinsed them perfunctorily and absently positioned them in the dishwasher.

After wiping the stove and countertops clean, Susan grabbed her jacket and headed for the front door to take their beagle for his morning walk.

"C'mon, Mutsy," she called. "Let's go, fella."

At that exact moment the front door opened on the house next door. Betty stepped out followed by her Newfoundland, Pete. The two women reached the sidewalk at the same time.

Their eyes met. All Susan could see was a lesbian, and all Betty could see was a judge.

They abruptly turned away from each other and walked in opposite directions.

DEMISE OF COURAGE

What keeps us from building loving, honest bridges to our neighbors and coworkers? What hinders our being forthright about spiritual issues even in our churches? What do we fear?

There is an insidious move afoot in our country to proclaim every kind of spiritual pursuit as equally valid—from witchcraft to New Age, from paganism to atheism. *Courage has taken a perverse journey from defending truth and convictions of integrity to protecting evil and the corruption within our culture.* Insistence that there is only one true God will be labeled not only politically incorrect, but intolerant.

In situation ethics there are no absolutes. We are given permission to make up our own code of morality—and woe unto the person who dares intimate that we should feel guilty about the code we have designed.

THE NEW VIRTUE

Tolerance is the new "virtue" as we approach the turn of the twenty-first century. It seeks to define and dictate the attitudes and actions of our contemporary culture. All others are passé.

Tolerance is the logical result of situation ethics which says that the rightness of any action depends upon whether it helps us or harms us at the time. Whether an action is moral or not is left up to us to decide. The rightness of the action can change from situation to situation and there is no objective way to measure it.

If we speak up against sin, we will be considered not only outdated but "evil," because we are rudely violating others' *right* to behave as they deem will make them happy at the moment. Blatant wickedness has become a brave stand for rugged individualism—always a noble note to sound in this country. However, if we condone wickedness through our "tolerance," we are asking righteousness to be a willing bedfellow with depravity.

DEADLY HESITATION

Meanwhile, Satan has not only trapped men and women in terrible sin, but attempts to tie the hands of anyone who could *rescue* them. There is great hesitation—if not fear—on the part of pastors and leaders to proclaim the morality of the Bible from their pulpits and platforms. We in the pews and on the streets are allowing ourselves as well to be influenced by what is "politically correct" and have become a very uncertain people when it comes to right and wrong.

In self-protection we have cocooned ourselves from the world. We no longer reach out with the message of salvation. We supposedly stay to ourselves so as not to offend, but the real motive is fear of a world whose values are gradually seeping into our own. We seek that one remaining "virtue" touted by the world—tolerance—while we watch a world go to hell and do nothing about it.

THE NEEDY CONFUSED BY OUR COWARDICE

A young woman recently told me how she had lived as a lesbian for six years next door to a Christian couple. They never once reached out to her in love to build a relationship through which they could have shared the gospel. At the time she knew only what the world told her—that her lifestyle was "normal." She couldn't understand why she was in such torment, why she hated herself and wished to die.

Years later she heard the gospel and accepted Jesus' love and forgiveness for her sin. She forgave those who had molested her as a child and who had set into motion the lesbian pattern of sin in her life. God has restored her life and she loves Him dearly. She is now married and in Bible school.

But she has had a hard time understanding how that Christian couple who lived next door had been able to watch her suffer and say *nothing* for six long years.

REVIVAL

Many Christians are fervently praying for revival to engulf this country. It is our only hope. If we humble ourselves as the Holy Spirit convicts—repenting of our cowardice and fear of man—we will find ourselves free of the shadows that paralyze us. Our eyes will be opened to see sin for the horror it is, and we will be moved with compassion for the lost.

FEARLESS DEVOTION

When the holiness of God overcomes us and we are broken again by what Jesus did for *us* at Calvary, our fear of the world will end. When we rise from our knees in humility and break the silence, there will be hope again for America.

And if we are persecuted for our "outrageous" stand, I pray that we will prove—to the death if necessary—our devotion to Christ and our love for those around us. Then, by the grace of God, when Christ returns He will not find us lurking in the shadows of cowardice. Instead, He will find a courageous, radiant Church that has kicked in the gates of hell and set the captives free!

PART 3:

FINAL VICTORY

CHAPTER SIXTEEN

EMBRACING REPENTANCE

Create in me a pure heart, O God,
and renew a steadfast spirit within
me.
Do not cast me from your presence
or take your Holy Spirit from me.
Restore to me the joy of your salvation
and grant me a willing spirit, to
sustain me. (Psalm 51:10-12)

The beautiful Bathsheba came at David's request. Perhaps she had loved him from a distance for years; perhaps not. But once she was within his reach behind closed doors, quiet conversation moved to passion with only a single touch. She slipped away from the palace as the sun's rays began stealing through the tall, half-shuttered windows of the royal bedchamber. David drifted between dark dreams, tossing restlessly.

During the following days, David busied himself with palace duties and the governing of the nation. But at night his sin replayed before his eyes, now without ecstasy—only horror.

How he wished he had gone with his men to battle! What a fool he had been! The poet-king's lyre lay still and no music stirred his heart day or night. His spirit was desolate. "My God, what have I done?" David cried out as he sought the Lord day after day.

But all was silent. The worst had arrived: God would not speak to him. He was alone with his sin.

Worship became futile and painful. As he knelt and tried to pray, the Seventh Commandment—written by the finger of God on the stone tablets concealed in the Ark which he loved—burned into his soul relentlessly.

Each day he tried to persuade himself that no one would know or care about his affair that night. The courier seemed to have forgotten his midnight mission, and the watchman never again mentioned David's inquiry after her. He seemed to be in the clear.

But try as he might, he could not breathe freely anymore. The air always seemed clotted around him. He never felt refreshed; his heart thundered within him at each recurring memory of that night.

One sin led to another when he found that Bathsheba carried his child. The adulterer turned to betrayal of an old and faithful friend . . . and then to murder.

SIN REVEALED

When the prophet Nathan confronted the king with his sins, David broke. Through sleepless nights and the fire of conviction, the Holy Spirit had been preparing him for this moment so that he would burst free from the chains of guilt in sweet repentance.

David knew that he alone was responsible. He blamed no one else. As Nathan fully revealed his sin, David's ready heart surrendered. In great relief he cried out to God for forgiveness and mercy, facing head-on what he had done and how he had broken the heart of God.

Why was it such a clear-cut matter for David to repent?

HIS LOVE OF GOD'S PRESENCE

Early in life, out on the rugged slopes with his sheep, David had sought the Maker of heaven and earth. He hadn't brushed off the awe that gripped him as the sun set in flaming orange and red upon the desert floor. He knew that the poignant melodies that poured from his heart and through his lyre had been sung first by the God who loved him and mysteriously kept him company.

When stories were told late at night back in his father's house in Bethlehem about Jehovah's marvelous deeds in centuries gone by, he didn't yawn and doze off. His heart leapt at the thought of a God so gentle that he watched over baby Moses in the bulrushes, yet so powerful that He could part the Red Sea.

So when he sinned, he knew that it was against not only the heavenly Lover of his life, but the mighty One of Israel, the King of all there is! Sin was no small thing to God—this David knew. It pierced the heart of the One who had placed a holy seal upon his own heart in covenant. This was something to reckon with in great humility and sorrow.

To lose God's presence? The thought was *death* to him. *(Taken from Second Samuel 11-12:1-13; Psalm 51.)*

GOD IS STILL HOLY

Do we, so many centuries removed from David's day, realize that God has not changed? Do we see that the covenant we embraced at salvation is surely as binding and significant for us now as it was for David?

It scares me that we think we are promised tomorrow and therefore can do today as we please. It scares me that we fight harder to preserve bitterness, resentment, image and control of our lives than to find time alone with the One who died for us. But that can change as our loneliness deepens and our longing for His presence grows.

GOD SHARES HIS HEART

The hunger that we feel in our hearts is—as all good things are—from our Father in heaven. He is sharing His heart with us. We are *first* feeling His hunger for us and then responding with hunger for *Him*.

He initiates the hunger, and He provides the way to return to intimacy with Him. He longs to help us stop drifting away.

DANGER AHEAD

"Honey," Janie whispered to her husband just before he drifted off to sleep, "I want to quit my job at the Girls' Home."

Martin was suddenly wide awake. "Why on earth do you want to do that?" He propped himself up on one elbow, scowling. "We can't afford for you to quit."

It took all the courage she had to continue. "Marty, my boss is coming on to me . . . and I'm feeling vulnerable," she ended weakly.

"Hey, c'mon. You're the strong one in this family," he stated dryly. "You're the 'spiritual giant.'

Besides, isn't your boss a 'man of God'?" His mouth shaped the words as though they tasted bad on his tongue.

Martin lay back down and rolled over, turning his back to her. "You can deal with it. We need the money," he muttered. A few minutes later he was asleep.

But Janie remained awake, an aching, foreboding fear seizing her spirit.

Martin seemed to care nothing for her life—as though she were so undesirable that no one could possibly be a threat to him. Or, she wondered with horror, did he *want* her to have an affair so that he could get out of the marriage?

She felt uncovered, unprotected, weak and undefended. How she longed to see Marty become a Christian! Surely then they could reconcile their differences and become "one."

The next morning Chris was waiting at the entrance of the Home for her. As she walked up, he gallantly swung the door wide open and bowed with a sweep of his arm, motioning her inside.

"After you, lovely lady," he cheerfully greeted her. As she hesitantly smiled and passed by him, his hand lightly touched her shoulder. A hunger for more jumped in her chest. His touch was tender and gentle, just like his voice—so different from Martin's cold and indifferent tone.

Chris *listened* to her. He listened as she shared her sorrows and dreams with him. Never had anyone leaned so close emotionally to hear her heart's cry as did this man. After years of struggling to understand and be understood in her marriage, the moments with Chris were like spring rain on her dreary, withered spirit.

Within two weeks of her appeal to Martin to help her escape, she was in a hotel room with Chris.

CRIPPLED WITH GUILT

When I met Janie, she was in the middle of the affair. The alternating agony and exhilaration of the relationship was tearing her apart. At the same moment that she felt more loved and cherished than ever in her life, she was dying from the inside out. She was struggling desperately to regain contact with the God she had loved and served for many years, while clinging to the poison of adultery.

It was taking a toll on her physically as well as spiritually. Her lovely hands were becoming twisted from arthritis that had set in when the affair started. It was as though her body, as well as her spirit, was crying out for her to stop the destruction. She was caught in the crossfire and being warned in every possible way.

GOD'S COMPASSION

As we finally prayed together, Jesus let her feel His arms around her once again, and she wept with sorrow for what she had done. But it was a tremendous struggle for her to get to the place of willingness to allow God to show her what was really going on. She so wanted to believe that the love between her and Chris was somehow pure, even if their behavior wasn't.

Then the Holy Spirit lifted the deception, and she saw their love for what it was. First, Chris's hold on her was based on manipulation and selfishness. He didn't love her for her sake at all! *If he had, he would never have led her into sin that destroyed her peace with God.*

Then she realized that they were both using each other to try to heal wounds in their lives that only God could heal. And it couldn't be done. Instead they were stripping the heart out of each other and destroying the glory that had been on their lives. Intimacy with God was impossible for either of them.

On her knees, tears streaming down her face, Janie repented and released her heart once again to the Lord. It was an amazing transaction.

THE FALLOUT

When Janie broke off the affair with Chris the next day, he was devastated and threatened suicide in an attempt to regain control. But she somehow held firm.

She confessed her sin to Martin and asked him to forgive her and go for marriage counseling with her. But his response was to treat her with more disdain than ever. After a few months of verbal abuse, he left her for someone else, saying smugly that he now had grounds for divorce.

Janie is building a new life in a little apartment by herself. With her eyes fixed on Jesus, she is slowly gaining strength and purpose in a world that sin had turned upside down.

There are still moments of deep sorrow over the past, but God is quietly etching His image upon her life as she humbly trusts in Him for the future. Not surprisingly, an amazing grace for counseling others who suffer from marital unfaithfulness or are tempted to look for love in all the wrong places has grown within her heart.

LONGING FOR THE FIRE

Even in the midst of rebellion, something in each of us longs for the fire of conviction. We yearn to surrender at the cross and have our lives cleansed once more—no matter what the fallout. We miss our Lord, and that pain outweighs any other.

We can still remember the joy of repentance when we first came to Jesus—the relief in confession, the bliss in forgiveness. We can recall the hunger we had for His Word and the ease with which we communed with Jesus as our best Friend. The excitement and downright reasonableness of sharing what He had done for us are sweet memories.

IT'S NOT TOO LATE

We *can* return to the cross. That's where the journey back to Him starts. No matter how far we have drifted from trusting Him to deliver us from our sorrows and fill our loneliness, we can be washed again in the blood of the Lamb. No matter how dreadfully we have been wronged, the cross can teach us how to forgive and release the pain to Him. No matter what our position is in the Body of Christ—pastor, worship leader, choir member, missionary, teen leader, Sunday school teacher, or even if we haven't been to church for a long, long time—His blood is waiting to cleanse us, and His love will be more than enough to heal our broken hearts.

His will is that we experience joy in His presence every single day. His commandments are given not to spoil our fun but to protect us from what He knows will destroy us. We were not designed for sin; nothing will go well when we travel that route.

He *will* fulfill His plans for us—if we will let Him.

Blessed Relief

Confession and repentance are not the horror that Satan would like us to believe. The cold sweat into which we break when we anticipate coming clean is *not* a premonition of agony; it is merely the flesh's last bid for control.

As we surrender in the crossfire of conviction and plead no case, but rather cry for mercy and forgiveness, the power of the flesh is broken. Life *can* be set right again. We *can* renew our covenant of love with Him, and the blood of Jesus will flow over our sins. We *can* be clean and again hear His voice clearly as in days long ago!

When we surrender our sin and acknowledge that Jesus Christ is Lord—even if the world has fallen down around us—we can finally breathe freely again. As we fall upon our faces in humility, that old rebel Pride is reduced to a shadow which the light of His presence promptly drives away. We are free.

We learn that to be washed in forgiveness and healed of our bitterness, with our wills realigned to His will, restores our joy and takes us into His presence.

"Oh, God!" we cry, "how I have missed You! How dear You are, how gentle Your touch, how pure Your gaze upon my life! How patient and merciful you have been! How I love You, Lord!"

As the tears of relief flow down our cheeks, His voice whispers to our hearts, "I love you too. Welcome home."

CHAPTER SEVENTEEN

COMPLETELY YIELDED

I eagerly expect and hope that I will in no way be ashamed, but will have sufficient courage so that now as always Christ will be exalted in my body, whether by life or by death. For to me, to live is Christ and to die is gain. (Philippians 1:20-21)

Shock swept over Simon's face, followed by consternation and then disdain. *What fool of a servant let this woman into my home?* His lips curled in derision as she fell at Jesus' feet and wept. The other guests were speechless.

But Jesus showed no surprise. As the tears fell upon His unshod feet, her brokenness touched His heart. She surrendered her life right there in the Pharisee's house. He rejoiced that she understood—as so few did—that He would gather up and cover even the vilest of sins and fill her with His inexpressible love. As she wept out her wounds and rebellion, her thirsty heart drank His forgiveness.

Doesn't the Man know what kind of woman this is? Simon wondered, pleased that apparently Jesus wasn't as perceptive as most people thought He was. For a moment Simon felt smugly above Jesus, relieved that he need not humble himself before this supposed Christ after all.

The drama continued. After tenderly wiping the tears from His feet with her hair, she pulled from beneath her robe a slender alabaster jar. Without a word or a look at Jesus' face, she began to pour its contents slowly over His feet.

Simon gasped. This was altogether too brazen for any woman to do in his house, much less a "lady of the night." *Jesus is mad to accept such attention!* he fumed to himself.

But Jesus said not a word. He graciously accepted her gift, His eyes lovingly embracing the scene at His feet. The sweet scent of the perfume—a symbol of her love and complete surrender—filled the room, carried on a faint breeze from an open window.

She understands, Jesus smiled to Himself. *She understands so much more than Simon ever will.* The smile faded from His eyes, and sadness filled them. The blindness of those who should be the first to see always grieved Him.

Turning to His annoyed host—whose thoughts He could read at a glance—Jesus said, "Simon, I have something to tell you."

"Tell me, Teacher," the Pharisee guardedly replied. He knew of Jesus' reputation for telling stories that didn't turn out as one would expect.

Jesus began His story. "Two men owed money to a certain moneylender. One owed him five hundred denarii, and the other fifty. Neither of them had the money to pay him back, so he canceled the debts of both. Now which of them will love him more?"

Not wanting to be caught by a trick question, Simon answered cautiously, "I suppose the one who had the bigger debt canceled."

"You have judged correctly," Jesus said. Simon sighed with relief but maintained his guard.

Then Jesus turned toward the woman and said, "Do you see this woman? I came into your house, and you did not give Me any water for My feet.

But she wet them with her tears and wiped them with her hair."

Jesus focused on Simon, who had begun to squirm. "You did not give Me a kiss, but this woman, from the time I entered, has not stopped kissing My feet," He said.

Simon's face burned with embarrassment.

Jesus pressed on. "You did not put oil on My head, but she has poured perfume on My feet."

Simon's head drooped, but his jaw remained set. "Therefore, I tell you," Jesus continued, "Her many sins have been forgiven—for she loved much. But he who has been forgiven little loves little." *(Taken from Luke 7:36-50.)*

To Understand Our Need

Simon hadn't sinned less, but his need of forgiveness had escaped his understanding. Until he comprehended his dire condition, he would never truly love Jesus.

There is no other way for any of us to come to Jesus. We must first know that there is no good thing within us. When that is clear, we find an alabaster jar within our hands.

When we are ready to give up every claim to our own importance; when we no longer crave the worship of others; when we see our own sins as the greatest evil because they kept us from peace with God and broke His Son's heart—*then* we are ready to be filled with Him.

We find ourselves lost in His presence, becoming absorbed into His very nature. With arms gladly wrapped around every cross He asks us to carry, we discover that the burden is light.

And when we remember the price He paid for us, we empty the alabaster jar. We pour forth the love of a sacrificed life. Born of a divine exchange—His love for our lives—we gain everything and lose only misery.

We begin to live by the power of *His life* and we can't tell where our heart ends and His begins.

HIS PRESENCE IN PERSECUTION

"What courage this man has! What a pity to waste it on heresy!" Young Saul of Tarsus spoke quietly to his companion, another student of Judaism. The other nodded, shaking his head in wonder.

"And his name?" asked Saul.

"Stephen," his friend replied.

Just then Stephen's voice rose to a loud cry that cut through the heart of every religious Jew within hearing distance.

"You stiff-necked people, with uncircumcised hearts and ears! You are just like your fathers: You always resist the Holy Spirit." At this the audience began to bristle.

"Was there ever a prophet your fathers did not persecute?" Stephen defiantly shouted. "They even killed those who predicted the coming of the Righteous One! And now you have betrayed and murdered Him—you who have received the law that was put into effect through angels but have not obeyed it."

When they heard this, they literally ground their teeth at him, so great was their anger at being insulted.

But Stephen, ignoring the mounting fury and full of the Holy Spirit, turned his eyes expectantly toward heaven.

"Look!" he cried out to the crowd as though they could see and would at last understand. "I see heaven open and the Son of Man standing at the right hand of God!"

But they couldn't see, and the crowd's agitation suddenly burst into a roar of anger. They rushed at him and dragged him out of the city.

Saul and his companion followed amid the multitude watching the spectacle.

"Keep an eye on this while we teach this blasphemer a thing or two!" an angry voice shouted as he threw his coat at Saul's feet. Other garments joined the pile as men stripped down for the job ahead.

The incensed Jewish leaders grabbed up stones of every size from the roadside and began hurling them at Stephen with vicious fervor. The young dissident—instead of fleeing for his life—surprised everyone by remaining and praying rather than resisting.

Meanwhile, Saul added his heckling taunts to the clamor as the crowd called out for vengeance. The sickening sounds of rock against flesh and bone filled the air as the venomous barrage pounded Stephen's body.

As death was about to overtake him, the first martyr for Christ cried out, "Lord, do not hold this sin against them." Forgiving them as Jesus had forgiven from the cross His own executioners, Stephen breathed his last. *(Taken from Acts 7:51-60.)*

NO RESERVATIONS

Our ultimate response to the fire of the Holy Spirit in facing the cross is complete identification with Him. There will be no reservations, nothing withheld, no other agenda than obedience. Whether it is in life or death, we who are being called count it all joy to bear His name.

We will seek His face—not for how He can make our days more pleasant on this dusty planet, but because we have come to love Him more than life. In fact, this earth will have begun to recede beyond the horizon as we go the *other* way to enter His presence day after day.

We will be at peace with what He sends us. We will find that the Lord gives and the Lord takes away, and we will bless the name of the Lord. We will keep our hands open, careful never to hold onto earthly things so tightly that we wouldn't know how to live without them. We know that His grace will be sufficient for us.

FREE AT LAST

The thorny spikes of grudges and offenses have been gently plucked from our hearts by Jesus at the cross, and the Holy Spirit has become our oil of healing and comfort. Our sins have disappeared beneath distant waves as they sink to the bottom of the sea, forgotten by God. And we are free!

Worry about pleasing everyone around us has been replaced by the joy of pleasing God. The suffering of life provokes compassion for others rather than the disdain or fear from the "old days" when we cared only for ourselves. Reaching out to strangers with the life and love of Jesus Christ brings us joy beyond description. Our minds are at peace, and our thoughts finally make sense in the light of eternity.

Oh, the struggle is still there to let go of some supposed importance we think we should have from time to time, but as we surrender to His will once again, we hear His voice and contentment returns.

It is more than enough to know beyond a shadow of a doubt that Jesus loves us, that the Father rejoices over us, and that the Holy Spirit will enable us to complete the race in victory.

When rejection comes, as it surely will again and again, we know where to go for comfort and purpose—deep into His presence where He lifts the load from our hearts. We return to live by His life, not our own.

Miracles catch us by surprise, and demons tremble when we say the name of Jesus with authority. But our delight is in knowing that we are redeemed by the blood of the Lamb.

And if persecution comes in this country, as it has in other parts of the world, we will know that He bore it all ahead of us. He wasn't sorry, so neither shall we be, to suffer for His name.

Coming Again

Soon He will come for us as a Bridegroom for His bride. And as He lifts the veil from our faces, He will find *His own image* reflected in our eyes. Our Oneness with Him, born out of the times of surrender in the crossfire of the Holy Spirit's conviction, will be complete.

In Heaven

Our worship in heaven will have begun down here at the cross when we gave up all the other loves. And we will be able to join our voices with those of the angels, singing:

> Hallelujah!
> For our Lord God Almighty reigns.
> Let us rejoice and be glad
> and give him glory!
> For the wedding of the Lamb has
> come,
> and his bride has made herself ready.
> (Revelation 19:6-7)

If you would like the author to speak at your church, ministry, conference or retreat, please put your request in writing and send it to:

Joyce Strong
P.O. Box 58452
Raleigh, NC 27609